About this Learning Guide

Shmoop Will Make You a Better Lover*
*of Literature, History, Poetry, Life...

Our lively learning guides are written by experts and educators who want to show your brain a good time. Shmoop writers come primarily from Ph.D. programs at top universities, including Stanford, Harvard, and UC Berkeley.

Want more Shmoop? We cover literature, poetry, bestsellers, music, US history, civics, biographies (and the list keeps growing). Drop by our website to see the latest.

www.shmoop.com

Table of Contents

Introduction

In a Nutshell

Howards End is frequently viewed as the second-most-ambitious of E.M. Forster's novels (the most ambitious is generally admitted to be *A Passage to India*, in which Forster attempts to take on the question of the British Empire and its position in the world). This is not to say that *Howards End* doesn't take on a huge project in its own right: in it, Forster takes a crack at the "condition of England" novel, a genre that took off in the nineteenth century. As the name indicates, this kind of novel attempts to draw a fleshed-out picture of the social world of England and its many, many problems, often with the goal of sketching out some kind of change for the future.

Howards End, which Forster published in 1910, is sometimes viewed as the last of the great nineteenth century condition of England novels. Forster spreads his plot over a wide range of social classes and conditions, and demonstrates the fact that they're all inextricably connected, and that the strictly hierarchical social system of the now-dead Victorian period no longer applies. Forster's take on Edwardian society (the period that followed the Victorian) is critical but also hopeful, and proposes a possible future in which people do find ways to connect with each other despite their differences.

Why Should I Care?

Howards End is now over hundred years old, and it seems like a highly appropriate time to ponder its meaning for us today. On the surface, it doesn't seem like we've got much in common with the Schlegel and Wilcox families, and their troubles with the modernization of English society don't look like they've got anything in common with the über-post-modern world we live in today. However, if you look a little deeper, you might realize that the questions that E.M. Forster's asking about the England of 1910 aren't so very different from questions facing any nation today.

How so? Well, *Howard's End* basically demands that we rethink what it means to be English, and what it means to have a national identity at all in an age of imperial tensions and divisions. The novel's looking at the problem of reconciling different national identities or characters, despite the fact that the countries behind them are at odds (specifically, England and Germany). In our multicultural world, we're faced with the same challenging questions of identity every day – after all, in a country of immigrants, who among us doesn't have a complicated relationship with our own roots?

Forster's novel, however, idealistically suggests a solution that we can all strive for: basically, this all boils down to Margaret Schlegel's fervent desire to "Only connect!" The novel yearns for a world in which we all reach out and connect with each other, not only as representatives of our countries or our religions, but as members of the human race.

Summary

Book Summary

We begin by meeting two families, one rather odd, and one super conventional. The odd family is the Schlegels, three orphaned siblings – Margaret, Helen, and Tibby – of an academic, quirky, and liberal background. The ordinary family is the Wilcoxes, represented by Mr. and Mrs. Wilcox and their three children, Charles, Paul, and Evie. The Wilcoxes are wealthy and industrious, while the Schlegels inherited their money and spend most of their time talking about art, politics, and literature.

The two families encounter each other at various points, but things get awkward after Helen and Paul embarrassingly fall in and out of love over the span of 24 hours. However, Margaret and Mrs. Wilcox strike up an odd friendship, despite the awkwardness between the two clans, and before Mrs. Wilcox dies rather suddenly, she changes her will and leaves her beloved family home, Howards End, to Margaret. This upsets the Wilcoxes, who don't think that Margaret, a stranger, has any right to the house, so they ignore the change and go about their business.

Meanwhile, the Schlegels befriend a lower-middle class young man, Leonard Bast, who has ambitions of intellectualism, but is held back by his lack of funds (and by his trashy wife, Jacky). Leonard provides a kind of tragic counterpoint to the life of effortless bohemianism of the Schlegels, and to the businesslike, bustling Wilcoxes; instead, he's always yearning for more than is available to him. Through a rather complicated turn of events, Leonard loses his job as a clerk, and falls into even worse circumstances; this was caused by advice that Henry Wilcox gave the Schlegels, which they passed on to Leonard. Helen sees their young friend's fall as Henry's fault.

Against all odds, Henry and Margaret become friends – and then more than friends. They get married, despite the differences between the two of them. It later scandalously emerges that Leonard's lowbrow wife, Jacky, used to be Henry's mistress, and that he abandoned her abroad (contributing to her bottom-of-the-barrel social position), and Henry and Margaret have to work through the issues produced by this revelation. Helen and Margaret drift further and further apart as Margaret is absorbed into the Wilcox clan. Their relationship hits a low when Helen tries to get Henry to financially help the Basts (he refuses because of his former relationship with Jacky).

This is where things go a little crazy. Helen, caught up in her sympathy for Leonard, has an affair with him, the result of which is pregnancy. She flees to Germany, trying to hide her pregnancy from her family and friends, but ultimately is forced to return to England. There, Henry and Margaret ambush her at Howards End, where they discover the truth; Margaret forces Henry to forgive her sister for her scandalous affair, since she herself has forgiven him his (with Jacky). Charles, Henry's hot-headed son, accidentally kills Leonard with a sword (yep, you heard that right) for bringing shame upon the family, and is sentenced to prison for manslaughter.

It seems that everything is falling apart for the Wilcoxes and Schlegels – but, in fact, it's the beginning of a new life for them. Henry finally begins to sympathize and truly connect with other people, as Margaret's been encouraging him to do all along. In the end, the two of them, along with Helen and her baby, form a kind of new, unified family, out of the fragments of the old ones. We end up at Howards End, which Henry bequeaths to Margaret and her nephew, as a beautiful summer arrives, along with a tentative new hope for England.

Chapter 1

- The narrator informs us that we're starting with Helen's letters to her sister, Meg.
- The first letter describes a house – a nice, homey place surrounded by trees. Sounds pretty good to us.
- Helen's apparently there, visiting some wealthy friends: Mr. and Mrs. Wilcox and their children. She plans to return to London that Saturday, where Margaret is detained at home with their feeble brother, Tibby. Helen claims that vigorous men like Mr. Wilcox and his son, Charles, would be a good influence on Tibby.
- Helen describes the Wilcoxes, who sound like a nice family, albeit somewhat batty. They all love the outdoors, and occupy themselves there, despite their hay fever. The family is composed of Mrs. Wilcox, Mr. Wilcox, and three children, Charles, Evie, and the yet-to-arrive Paul.
- Helen's second letter reveals that she's been won over completely by the Wilcoxes – they're apparently totally different from the liberal, wacky Schlegels, and she's intrigued by this glimpse into their lifestyle. For once, Helen (who seems like quite an opinionated young lady) is "knocked into pieces" in conversation by Mr. Wilcox, and she enjoys it.
- Helen's third letter is short and dramatic – she is in love with Paul Wilcox.

Chapter 2

- Upon reading her sister's last letter, Margaret is understandably freaked out, and expresses her concern to her Aunt Juley. After all, the sisters don't even know the Wilcoxes that well – they'd met them traveling in Germany, and were both invited to come visit the family. Margaret, as we already know, couldn't go because of Tibby's illness.

- Margaret pauses to think and Aunt Juley takes over. She puts in her two cents about the encounter with the Wilcoxes in Germany (awkwardly insulting Germans, and by extension the Schlegels – she quickly covers it up by saying she thinks of them as English). She then pushes Meg gently about the Wilcoxes. Are they the right family for Helen? Do they care about the arts? Is marriage to Paul even possible?
- Both women start talking, trying to figure out what should happen. Aunt Juley suggests that Margaret go to the Wilcoxes' house and work things out herself.
- Then, Aunt Juley has another idea – why doesn't *she* go to see about this business herself instead of Margaret?
- Margaret refuses, saying that she will go to Howards End (the house), and promises Aunt Juley that she won't offend anyone by asking too many questions.
- Aunt Juley says that the engagement must be broken off – slowly. We're not sure what that means, exactly, and neither is Margaret. She tries to convince her niece once more that she should go instead.
- Margaret thanks her aunt, then goes to check on Tibby, who's not at all well. Margaret feels obliged to stay with her brother, and changes her mind – Aunt Juley will go to Howards End after all, under strict instructions not to bring up the engagement to anyone but Helen.
- Margaret and Aunt Juley set off for the train station at King's Cross, and Margaret ponders the sense of infinity and possibility that the station gives off. Aunt Juley departs, but when Margaret gets home, she discovers an urgent telegram from Helen, saying that everything is over with Paul – and that she shouldn't tell anyone anything. Well, it's too late for that.

Chapter 3

- Aunt Juley (or rather, Mrs. Munt, as she's called for the most part in this chapter) thinks over her mission, and over her nieces' history as she travels.
- We learn that the three Schlegel children lost their mother when Tibby was born, when the girls were both pretty young. They were raised by their German father, who died five years later. Margaret has been in charge of the family ever since, and handles everything, including their financial matters.
- Helen and Margaret are both very independent women; they're friends with all kinds of interesting artistic types and foreigners, which rather alarms their aunt.
- The train travels north through the countryside, and deposits Mrs. Munt at the village of Hilton, where Howards End is located.
- In the station, an employee hooks Aunt Juley up with a certain Mr. Wilcox, who's on his way to Howards End. She asks if he's the older or younger Mr. Wilcox; when he replies the younger, she assumes that he's Paul (Helen's supposed lover).
- The young man offers to drive her to Howards End, and she accepts. In the car, she goes against Margaret's command and brings up the engagement.
- This is a BIG mistake, seeing as this isn't *actually* Paul, but is instead his older brother,

Charles (who's still technically the "younger" Mr. Wilcox, compared to his father). He's confused – then enraged.

- Charles goes into a fit, saying that the marriage is impossible. Mrs. Munt responds by being equally indignant. They fight the whole way back to Howards End, arguing about whose family is better than whose.
- At the house, Helen rushes up to tell her aunt that it's all over (Margaret sent a telegram to make sure that Helen knew what was coming).
- Paul comes out of the house, and Charles demands to know what's going on. Everyone is confused.
- Mrs. Wilcox shows up and stops the fighting. The narrator offers a fascinating description of her: she somehow knows exactly what to do to put everyone out of their misery. She soothes Charles, telling everyone that the engagement is off.

Chapter 4

- Back in the Schlegel home at Wickham Place, London, Helen and Aunt Juley both break down. Counting Tibby, Margaret has three people to take care of.
- Aunt Juley quickly forgets that she herself was largely the cause of the troubles at Howards End, and starts to look at the situation in a more positive light – she tells herself that she's done all she can to help her nieces.
- Helen, on the other hand, doesn't get over it quite so fast. Her whole life has been altered by the Wilcoxes, and it's hard for her to shake them off.
- For the first time, Helen was among people with ideas different from her own – while the Schlegels live sheltered, academic, liberal lives, the Wilcoxes are people of business, and their conservative ideas about the world are vastly different. Helen actually enjoyed arguing with them, even when they shot her down.
- Even before Paul arrived, Helen was ready to focus all of her love for the Wilcoxes on someone – and he was the right age and handsome enough, so she immediately allowed herself to fall in love with him.
- Paul himself was in a flirtatious mode; he was waiting to go earn some money through business in Nigeria and he basically had nothing to lose. So, to cut to the chase, he kissed Helen and told her he loved her.
- On Monday morning, though, things were different. As soon as Helen saw Paul in the morning, she noticed that he looked afraid – and for a man of the Wilcox sort, that's a pretty alarming thing.
- Helen, horrified, defused the situation (for the time being) by having a little chat with Paul – they agree that they'd been silly the night before.
- Helen gets Paul to send a telegram to Margaret for her, saying that there's nothing to worry about.
- However, as we know, Aunt Juley was already on her way, and her dramatic arrival with Charles troubles Helen.

- The Schlegels resolve to leave this episode behind them. They take up their ordinary lives again, entertaining interesting people and following liberal politics.
- The narrator gives us a little background on the Schlegel sisters. They're half-German and their father was a romantic figure – an idealistic, academic type. He didn't believe in the aggressive, imperial kind of Germany he saw emerging, so he moved to England and married an Englishwoman. There, he educated his children in his philosophical ways, which explains why Margaret and Helen are the way they are.
- Helen is prettier than Margaret, but similarly intelligent and forward. Margaret is more blunt than her sister and less of a social success.
- Tibby, their younger brother, doesn't merit much mention – he's a smart sixteen year old boy, but is somewhat persnickety and difficult.

Chapter 5

- The chapter opens on the scene of the extended Schlegel family attentively listening to a performance of Beethoven's Fifth Symphony, each in their own way.
- Helen romantically infuses the music with her own imagination, and sees a whole fantastical string of images that accompany it.
- Margaret hears only the music.
- Tibby, always academic, knowledgeably ponders the musical score as he listens.
- They are accompanied by their cousin Frieda Mosebach, her "young man," Herr Liesecke, and Aunt Juley.
- In between movements, Aunt Juley notices Margaret talking to an unknown young man, about whom she asks Helen. They're interrupted by the start of the second movement, the Andante.
- We are treated to the narrator's observations of these various listeners, all of whom have different ways of responding to the music. To whimsical Helen, the movement speaks of pessimistic goblins walking around the world, only to be blown away by Beethoven's ending (though they might always come back).
- Helen is overcome by the music, and she escapes during the applause to go home alone.
- The young man Margaret's speaking to pipes up, noticing that Helen has stolen his umbrella in her quick escape.
- Margaret tries to make Tibby run after Helen to fetch it, but he refuses. The next piece, the Four Serious Songs by Brahms, prevents anyone from going anywhere.
- When the Brahms ends, Margaret gives her calling card to the young man, in case he'd like to come by and pick up his umbrella after the concert. The two of them make small talk, and Margaret comments that she doesn't like the next piece in the concert program, Elgar's *Pomp and Circumstance*. At this, Frieda and Herr Liesecke dash away to go meet up with some friends, to Aunt Juley's dismay.
- Frieda leaves her bag behind, and the young man dashes out to give it to her. He feels good about the fact that Margaret trusted him with Frieda's purse, and decides to go with

the Schlegels to pick up his umbrella from their house after the concert.

- Margaret finds the young man quite intriguing, despite the fact that his over-eager manners make her feel their class difference (though it's not very distant), and she wants to invite him to tea. As they walk, they further discuss music, and Tibby and Aunt Juley steal the show, arguing about the music they've just heard.
- The discussion spreads to Margaret, who asks whether or not music and other art forms (particularly painting) are the same or different. Helen, apparently, believes them to be the same, while Margaret maintains that there's a difference. The young man is intrigued by these odd siblings in turn.
- Margaret goes on, trash talking German composer Richard Wagner for blending all of the arts together.
- The young man, meanwhile, is overwhelmed by this high-flown discussion. He can't imagine what it must be like to be as cultured and knowledgeable as Margaret. He then begins to worry about his umbrella – apparently, he's quite a worrier.
- The party arrives at Wickham Place, and Margaret asks the young man to come in and have some tea. He's distraught by this crazy family.
- Helen flies downstairs to let them into the house, and apologizes for taking the man's umbrella. Apparently, the inadvertent theft of other people's hats and umbrellas is pretty commonplace for Margaret and Helen. She finds a particularly ratty umbrella in their collection, and, though she says it must be hers, it's actually the young man's. He takes it and dashes off.
- Margaret blames Helen for scaring the stranger off, and she runs out to try and stop him, but it's no use. Aunt Juley thinks it's a good thing he left – after all, she reasons, he might have stolen some of the valuable knickknacks lying about the house, including a precious picture by the painter Charles Ricketts.
- Tibby is bored by this and goes upstairs to tend to the tea and scones. He's obviously an expert at this duty.
- On their way upstairs to join their brother, Helen remarks that she wishes they had a "real" boy in the house, not just the opera-loving Tibby. When they get to him, Margaret accuses Tibby of not making their visitor feel at home enough; the house, in her opinion, is too full of "screaming women." Tibby has no defense.
- They argue over what kind of man they should have around the house – Margaret teases Helen that they might be better off with some men like the "W."s (the Wilcoxes, that is).
- Margaret comes to the conclusion that their home is irrevocably feminine, but they should try and keep it from being effeminate, a fine distinction.
- The sisters laugh about the idea of stuffy Queen Victoria hosting a dinner party full of Pre-Raphaelite artists, and the conversation is derailed.
- Though they move onto other subjects, it's clear that the young man of the stolen umbrella left quite an impression.

Chapter 6

- We learn immediately that the young man with the umbrella's name is Leonard Bast. He's not exactly poverty-stricken yet, but he's also certainly not in the same class as the Schlegels. He's undernourished in every possible way – physically, intellectually, emotionally.
- Leonard feels like his pride is a little bruised as he walks away from the Schlegel's house; he decides that they're not real ladies after all.
- Leonard runs into a colleague from his job (he's a clerk), and walks home to the rather miserable-sounding street where he lives. He runs into another acquaintance, then arrives in his apartment.
- The place really doesn't sound too appealing, even though Forster tells us that it's "amorous" and "not unpleasant." Still, it has a seedy feel to it.
- Leonard knocks over a framed photo when he takes off his boots, and the glass breaks. The picture is of a girl called Jacky – in it, her smile is dazzling, but the narrator notes a certain anxiety in her eyes.
- Leonard cuts his finger and blunders about the flat (which he's renting furnished – it's not actually his stuff). He settles down to read *The Stones of Venice* by John Ruskin.
- Leonard tries to imitate Ruskin's style, and tries to truly understand Culture, just as he was in the concert.
- His reverie is interrupted by the arrival of a tackily dressed woman – a floozy, one might even say. It's Jacky, the woman from the photograph (though much older).
- Leonard and Jacky talk half-heartedly – obviously, their relationship is not an intellectual one.
- Jacky forces Leonard to tell her he loves her; he responds that he can't marry her until he's 21 in November (she's 33), but promises to keep his word.
- Leonard goes off on a tirade about how he's not one to leave a girl in the lurch, and about how he's on a campaign of self-improvement through Art and Literature.
- Jacky doesn't care about this. She just wants to know that he loves her.
- The couple sits down to a depressing dinner of basically artificial food.
- After supper, they chill awkwardly in the sitting room – it sounds horrifying. Leonard plays the piano badly and Jacky flees to bed. It doesn't take a genius to see that this is not a couple in love.
- Alone, Leonard ponders the Miss Schlegels. He's fascinated by them and jealous that he'll never be like them.
- Leonard continues with Ruskin, ignoring Jacky's calls for him to come to bed.

Chapter 7

- The next morning, Aunt Juley has some bad news – the Wilcoxes are moving into a new building across the street at Wickham Place.

- Aunt Juley, being more – well, for lack of a better word – *normal* than her nieces and nephew, always seems to be more up on the neighborhood gossip than they are, which is how she found out about the Wilcoxes.
- Aunt Juley and Margaret worry about the possibility of Helen running into Paul. They decide that the Schlegels must be very careful with their new neighbors. Helen laughs it off, and says that there's nothing to worry about.
- Frieda and Helen go to meet Bruno (Herr Liesecke), and Margaret and Aunt Juley continue to worry.
- Margaret expresses a theory (new to the metaphysical Schlegels, but old to the rest of the civilized world) that money makes everything easier – things couldn't possibly get too bad between the Wilcoxes and Schlegels because they are both wealthy, and they have their wealth to rely upon, even when other things fall through.
- Margaret and Aunt Juley go off on an errand (they notice Evie watching them from the Wilcox balcony as they go). Margaret worries that, between the meddling Frieda and Aunt Juley, Helen might be troubled again by the Wilcoxes.
- Just in case, Margaret checks in with Helen, who says that it's absolutely fine that the Wilcoxes are there – she's traveling with Frieda for a while anyway.

Chapter 8

- The narrator speculates as to the roots of the odd friendship of Mrs. Wilcox and Margaret Schlegel, which perhaps began before they even recognized it, when they first met in Germany.
- Mrs. Wilcox unintentionally makes trouble at Wickham Place by calling on the Schlegels. Margaret and Helen aren't sure what to do – Margaret is especially concerned. Should she return the visit or not? How can they possibly be friends, given what's happened with Helen and Paul?
- Margaret writes a letter telling Mrs. Wilcox that they shouldn't meet, just in case. Mrs. Wilcox immediately writes back to say that Paul has gone abroad, and Margaret instantly feels bad about her rejection of the other woman.
- Margaret dashes off across the street to apologize in person. She's shown up to Mrs. Wilcox's bedroom, where they assure each other that there's no danger of Paul and Helen meeting.
- They briefly discuss the Paul and Helen situation; Margaret wants to know how Mrs. Wilcox could tell that the young pair had fallen for each other. No answer is given.
- Margaret makes like she's going to leave when the maid stops in to take away Mrs. Wilcox's breakfast tray, but she's invited to stay, and they chat a bit about Charles's recent wedding to Dolly, a pretty but silly young woman.
- The talk turns to Howards End, and Mrs. Wilcox tells Margaret about a curious superstition – there's a set of hog's teeth stuck in the bark of the big wych elm tree at the house, and the locals think that chewing on a piece of bark will cure toothache. Margaret is intrigued.

- It turns out that Howards End belongs to Mrs. Wilcox herself, not her husband – she was actually born there.
- As the chatter moves away from Howards End, Margaret gets bored. She accidentally breaks a picture frame, and makes her excuses to go back home.
- Mrs. Wilcox and Margaret say goodbye, and as they do, Mrs. Wilcox says rather an odd thing – she reminds Margaret that she's still just a "girl" (of 29), and is inexperienced. Margaret responds by admitting that she has a lot to learn, but she's already discovered that life is complicated and unexpected.

Chapter 9

- Margaret, it is revealed, wasn't being entirely honest with her new friend – in fact, she thinks of herself as quite experienced.
- Even so, she isn't experienced enough to foresee the disaster that arrives when she throws a luncheon party for Mrs. Wilcox. She invites some usual Schlegel guests over; these clever people with their witty, whimsical conversations are too much for Mrs. Wilcox, and she finds herself with nothing to contribute beyond small talk.
- Margaret and her friends chatter on and on, but Mrs. Wilcox doesn't fit in with them at all. She makes herself rather unpopular with some old-fashioned statements about a woman's proper place, and excuses herself early. All the same, Margaret has the odd feeling that there's something more to her new friend than meets the eye (her old friends don't agree).

Chapter 10

- After several days, Margaret worries that she and Mrs. Wilcox will never become close friends.
- Then, just as Margaret is despairing, Mrs. Wilcox asks her to go Christmas shopping.
- The two of them drive around all day, looking for Christmas presents. Margaret describes a typical Schlegel family Christmas, and mentions in passing that they'll be moving soon.
- Apparently, the Schlegels will be forced to move out of Wickham Place in a few years, when their lease is up, despite the fact that they've lived there their whole lives.
- Mrs. Wilcox chats with an acquaintance as Margaret efficiently helps her pick out some new Christmas cards.
- As they return to their carriage, Mrs. Wilcox brings up the house again – she's clearly troubled by the fact that the Schlegels are going to be turned out. It emerges that the Wickham Place house is going to be demolished to make room for new flats; if Howards End were ever pulled down, Mrs. Wilcox would freak out. She gets carried away and asks Margaret to come to Howards End with her right then.

- Margaret makes an excuse, and they return to Wickham Place – clearly, no was not the right answer. The atmosphere is decidedly awkward. Mrs. Wilcox attempts to make small talk, but now Margaret feels upset, too. They drive home in uncomfortable silence.
- Back at Wickham Place, Margaret feels awful. How come she didn't say yes when Mrs. Wilcox asked her to come to Howards End?
- Tibby, contrarily, sees that his sister is feeling quiet, so he feels like talking all of a sudden. He jabbers on and on, while Margaret agonizes about her missed opportunity to see the famous Howards End. As soon as lunch is over, she goes across the street, but finds that Mrs. Wilcox has left for the night.
- She goes to the train station to see if she can find Mrs. Wilcox – as she's buying a ticket to Hilton to find Howards End, the two friends find each other, and it's decided that they'll go spend the night at the house.
- As they're about to leave, though, they run into two unexpected arrivals – Evie and Mr. Wilcox are back early from their driving trip in Yorkshire, due to a car crash. The trip to Howards End is postponed.

Chapter 11

- In an abrupt shift, we find ourselves leaving a funeral. We see the attendees milling around, and learn that this is a Wilcox family funeral, in Hilton – it turns out to be Mrs. Wilcox's. We see the goings on from the perspective of a wood-cutter, who's saddened by the events.
- The people of the village obviously cared for Mrs. Wilcox, and for her husband, as well. Charles, however, is not as popular. There's a sense that the younger generation is somehow worse than their parents.
- The wood-cutter keeps working as the people drift away, and, even though he disapproves of colored flowers at a funeral, takes one of the flowers from the grave and leaves (he later regrets not taking all of the flowers, since it freezes over that night).
- At Howards End, the whole family is in mourning. Mr. Wilcox is overcome with memories of his dead wife's goodness and innocence, and he can't believe that she's gone – she didn't tell him of her illness, and died rather suddenly.
- Evie comes in with the day's mail; she wants to help, but she's not sure what to do.
- She goes back to Charles and Dolly, and Charles goes in to see their father next. He's equally unsuccessful at getting Mr. Wilcox to eat anything, but pretends to be in charge.
- Dolly, Charles's new wife, is useless. She's frivolous and unfeeling, and she can't help but wish that Mrs. Wilcox had died before the wedding, so she wouldn't have to be in mourning.
- Charles, Dolly, and Evie embark on some trivial conversation about the trees in the village – they can't face up to their real sorrow. It's the Wilcox way to avoid things that are deeply felt, even though they are truly sad at heart.
- Even obnoxious Charles is full of feelings; everything around the house reminds him of his

mother. Evie is also struck by her mother's absence, not just in the house, but in her life. As the narrator sadly comments, the children's sadness is different from their father's, for "a wife may be replaced; a mother never."

- Charles thinks over his mother's will, which seems fair enough – all of her things are divvied up between her husband and children (Mr. Wilcox will get Charles End, and Charles will get it after him).
- Charles decides that he and Dolly will return to London so he can go back to work, because to stick around Howards End would be too depressing.
- Charles heads down to the garage, notices that there's some mud on his new car, and harasses the chauffeur for a while. While they're talking, Dolly comes out and tries (incoherently) to communicate something strange to him: Miss Schlegel (Margaret, that is), "has got" Howards End.
- Everyone's all in a tizzy. Mr. Wilcox tries to clear things up by explaining: he's received a letter from the matron of the nursing home where Mrs. Wilcox died, in which a note from Mrs. Wilcox is enclosed. The note says that she wants Margaret to inherit Howards End.
- The whole family is taken aback. Dolly foolishly tries to intervene, but is told not to meddle.
- The note isn't legal, but that's not the issue. Mr. Wilcox clearly wants to do what is most loyal to the memory of his wife; Charles, on the other hand, thinks that Margaret must have interfered somehow in her own interest (he assumes that everyone is as selfish as he is).
- The family deliberates for hours. The narrator steps in here and agrees that the Wilcoxes shouldn't give the house to Margaret, since the last minute change isn't legal – and, after all, it communicates something about their mother that they couldn't understand. To Mrs. Wilcox, the act was spiritual; Howards End was more than just a house to her, and she saw Margaret as a kindred spirit and an heir to what the house represents. To her husband and children, though, Howards End is simply an asset.
- This final bequest seems treacherous to the Wilcoxes – they can't believe Mrs. Wilcox would do such a thing. They decide that the whole thing isn't at all like her, and dismiss it. There's more talk about Margaret – none of the Wilcoxes seem to like her, and Charles and Dolly put her down for sending the scandalous colored chrysanthemums, and even for coming to the funeral. They attribute her oddness to the fact that she's not "really English," but is instead a "German cosmopolitan." Mr. Wilcox puts his foot down and says that they are not to blame her, since she was just as in the dark about all of this as they were.
- Charles brushes the incident off and diverts the conversation back to his new car and the chauffeur. It seems like this troublesome interlude is over.

Chapter 12

- It turns out that Margaret didn't know about Mrs. Wilcox's bequest after all. She feels undone by her friend's death, and contemplates the way in which she disappeared from the world.
- Margaret also thinks over the funeral – it was nothing but a ceremony, with nothing to do

with Mrs. Wilcox's actual death.

- Finally, she also thinks a lot about the Wilcoxes, who she can't understand; they live in a completely different world than her family, and she can't blame them for it (the way Helen and Tibby do).
- Margaret and Helen exchange letters (the latter is still in Germany). Helen is unaffected by Mrs. Wilcox's death – she's a little sad, but that's it.
- Helen returns from Germany, and has had another marriage proposal, which she rejected. The Schlegels' cousin Frieda keeps trying to set them up with potential German spouses to bring them back to their original homeland.
- Tibby also has news – he's getting ready to go to Oxford, and he loves it for its aesthetic qualities. We get the feeling again that Tibby is rather an odd duck.
- Margaret interrupts the pleasant family banter to bring up the Wilcoxes. We can tell from what she says that they made an effort to see if Mrs. Wilcox had told Margaret about leaving Howards End to her – obviously she didn't, and obviously they're not going to tell her. Mr. Wilcox ended up giving Margaret a silver vinaigrette (an ornate box, not a salad dressing) to remember Mrs. Wilcox by.
- Helen isn't interested. She pauses to be polite, then goes on talking about her Germany trip.
- Margaret sees that life isn't as linearly organized as history makes it seem; one can never really be prepared for things. She resolves to be less cautious in the future.

Chapter 13

- Two years pass. The Schlegels go about their business as usual, in the midst of a changing cityscape – London is getting bigger and badder.
- The narrator goes off on a little diatribe about the development of the city; he's distraught by the changes wrought by modern times.
- Margaret is also distraught – the lease on Wickham Place is finally up, which means they have to find a new house.
- Tibby is visiting from Oxford, and Margaret takes the opportunity to ask him his opinion, both about the house situation and about his future. He has no answers to either question.
- It turns out that Tibby doesn't want to do anything at all in life, even though Margaret holds up two examples of their acquaintances who don't have professions, and don't seem happy.
- Tibby complains, but Margaret presses on, saying that all men (and, she thinks, women in the future) should work. Margaret likes men in general much better than women, and Tibby distracts her by asking why she doesn't just get married.
- Margaret says that her proposals all came from "ninnies" – men who didn't have anything else to do (oh snap!). She emphasizes the importance of work (or at least *seeming* like you work) to Tibby, and brings up the example of the Wilcoxes, who she claims are "the right sort."

- Margaret has more traditional views than her brother or sister, and thinks that the Wilcox urge to earn money and do one's duty is a good thing. Neither Tibby nor Margaret care much for what London has become, but she admires the activity that goes into it.
- They abandon the futile subject of Tibby's career, and go back to house hunting. It's clear that they should stay in London, but Helen and Margaret thought that they might get a house in the country and keep a flat in the city.
- Helen busts into the room in a tizzy. Apparently, there's been some excitement downstairs – a woman came by seeking her husband.
- The siblings wonder if it's Bracknell, a newly employed servant, but it seems that it's not. Who could it be?
- Helen can't believe how hilarious this is. She calls the mystery woman "Mrs. Lanoline" (on account of her husband's name being either Lan or Len). Nobody knows why she thought her husband was at Wickham Place, but she insists that she has her reasons.
- Helen advised Mrs. Lanoline to go to the police, and she leaves – but Helen's sure that she suspected the Schlegels all along of...something.
- To Helen this is all a joke to write to Aunt Juley about, but Margaret is worried that it might be something more serious. Margaret worries about leaving Wickham Place. What will await them out in the city? The whole episode leaves a bad taste in her mouth.

Chapter 14

- The next day, the mystery of Mrs. Lanoline is solved. Her missing husband turns out to be our old friend, Leonard Bast, who stops by to explain about his wife's visit.
- The three Schlegels rush down, and though they expect a gallivanting philanderer, they instead find a downtrodden, pale young man. He has the air of someone who's been crushed by the city, though he should have grown up healthy and happy in the countryside.
- Leonard explains that he still had Margaret's calling card from that fateful meeting at the concert two years ago – the Schlegels don't remember him. He says that he'd told his wife that he had a call to make, and she found the card and assumed that he was visiting Wickham Place.
- Helen pushes further; it's obvious that he hasn't told them the whole truth.
- It emerges that Leonard left home Saturday afternoon, but Mrs. Bast came looking for him Sunday afternoon. It all looks very fishy.
- Leonard sees that the Schlegels assume the worst about him, and wants to clear his name. He asks if they've read a number of books that he finds inspirational, but Helen and Tibby have no patience for this literary justification – they (and we) want to know what he was really up to.
- Apparently the answer is simple: he walked. And walked. And walked. Leonard walked all alone, all night.
- At this point, Tibby gives up and leaves, but his sisters are enthused by the idea. They ask for the details – apparently he started in Wimbledon, and went through the woods, off the

road. The women are impressed.

- Leonard walked until dawn, found a train station, and took a train back to London. Unfortunately, the dawn was not as beautiful as poets would have us believe.
- Leonard tries to explain what he was feeling as this all happened – mostly hungry and tired – but also determined. He's certain that there must be more to life than simply going to the office and living a limited existence. Overwhelmed, he retreats to his literary heroes, not fully understanding that there's something in *him* that doesn't just come from his reading.
- Margaret and Helen reassure their new friend that they don't think he was being foolish – rather, they think his adventure was marvelous.
- The Schlegels invite Leonard back, but he refuses, saying that this talk has been one of the best things in his life, and he doesn't want to spoil it.
- Leonard rushes away, intoxicated by his interaction with these fascinating people.
- We hear a bit about Leonard and Jacky's dull, unhappy marriage; apparently, Margaret's calling card has been a point of contention for the last two years. For Jacky, it's an infuriating mystery, while for Leonard (who never told her how he got it in the first place), it's a symbol of the kind of life he longs for, that Jacky will never understand.
- When Leonard returned home Sunday night, he found the card missing, figured out what his wife was up to, and taunted Jacky by saying that he knows where she has been (to see the Schlegels), but she doesn't know what he's been up to. She halfheartedly demands an explanation, but he offers none to her.
- Leonard walks home from Wickham Place gleefully, feeling as though his life has changed. He realizes that – shock and horror! – he's forgotten to put his hat on, and people are staring. He dons it, and continues on his way, with no outward sign of his inner turmoil showing.

Chapter 15

- Helen and Margaret are also struck by their experience with Leonard, and they can't stop talking about him to their friends at dinner that night. They keep finding ways to bring him up in conversation, even in relation to a paper on philanthropy that's being presented that evening.
- "Mr. Bast" becomes a stand-in for the lower classes in general, and everyone tries to decide what could be done to make his life better.
- The Schlegels and their companions argue about how to "educate" the poor; Margaret claims that money is the only thing necessary for education, and that everything else (culture, morality, etc.) follows from it.
- Everyone is shocked by this statement, but conversation goes on in a humorous and jovial fashion until the dinner guests leave, and the Schlegels walk home happily.
- The Schlegels stroll along the Thames embankment, and sit to look at the river. The sisters wonder if they should stay in touch with Leonard.
- Margaret brings up the problem of their housing situation and mentions Mrs. Wilcox and

Howards End in passing. From a distance, Mr. Wilcox (who's sitting with some friends further down the embankment) hears his name and walks over – he recognizes the Schlegels and says hello. He sounds masculine and protective, seeing that they're two ladies sitting alone at night, and while Helen resents this, Margaret thinks it's fine.

- The two sisters chat politely with Mr. Wilcox, and Margaret inquires about Paul; the Wilcoxes have business concerns in the colonial world, and Mr. Wilcox politely evades some tension about England's competition with Germany (remember, this is right before World War I).
- Mr. Wilcox changes the topic and asks how they're doing; Helen tells him all about their evening with their debate club, and he's amused and charmed by their idealistic pastimes. We learn that he's become quite a powerful man over the past couple of years, and he's riding pretty high right now.
- Mr. Wilcox rather dismissively says that he wishes Evie would join a club like theirs, instead of breeding terriers (her new hobby).
- Helen responds rather irritably and defensively, and Mr. Wilcox tries to calm her down, saying that he agrees that debates are healthy and useful – he wishes he'd been more of a debater when he was younger, as being a bit quicker would be helpful to him now.
- Margaret diffuses the tension, and Helen laughs off her ill-temper. She changes the topic to Leonard, and tells Mr. Wilcox all about the argument their friends were having about how best to help him. The suggestions ran the gamut from simply giving him an annual income to sending him away for a holiday every summer. She asks Mr. Wilcox what *he* would do.
- Mr. Wilcox, ever the practical man, laughingly says he can't think of anything else beyond what's been suggested, except to tell him to leave his current employer (the Porphyrion Fire Insurance Company), since he knows that it's going to go under.
- Mr. Wilcox recommends that Leonard look for a new job now, while he's still employed, to avoid getting laid off later.
- The economy makes it very difficult for anyone to get a job these days (we know how *that* feels), and we have to wonder what Leonard could possibly do. Mr. Wilcox has no suggestions, and gets up to go back to his friends.
- As he's leaving, Margaret asks how Howards End is doing. We hear that the Wilcoxes have rented it out and moved away – they're worried that it's getting too suburban. Mr. Wilcox and Evie live in London with a country house in Shropshire, and Charles and Dolly still live in Hilton at another house.
- They part ways, and Margaret and Helen decide to share their advice about the Porphyrion Company with Leonard over tea.

Chapter 16

- Leonard comes over for tea the next weekend, but it doesn't go well at all. Helen and Margaret start asking him questions about his job, and he gets suspicious immediately.
- The women keep pushing the issue, asking if the Porphyrion is a good company. Leonard

gets irate.

- The fact of the matter is, he doesn't really know; to him, the company is like a giant, and he only does what the giant tells him to do.
- The sisters come right out and tell him that a friend has told them that the company is going to go bust. Leonard denies it – kind of. He gets flustered by the Schlegels and doesn't really say anything either way.
- Helen and Margaret continue to pursue the issue, and ask more and more questions. Leonard gets frustrated by the idea that they're wasting precious time talking about money, and he finally butts in with talk of books.
- Unfortunately, they're interrupted right away by Evie and Mr. Wilcox, who bustle in with two adorable puppies.
- Helen is captivated by the pups, which Evie bred and named Ahab and Jezebel.
- Leonard is not amused by this interruption, and makes to leave. Helen absently tells him to come again, and he can't stand this. He bluntly says no, he won't, since it would be a failure.
- This gets Helen's attention, and, insulted, she asks why he would say such a thing.
- Leonard and Helen yell at each other – he thinks they're patronizing him, and she thinks they just want to help.
- Leonard appeals to Mr. Wilcox, who agrees that it's not fair for him to show up to tea, only to have his "brain picked" by the Schlegels. Leonard thinks that the Schlegels only wanted to make use of him somehow to get inside information about the Porphyrion or something, and is highly insulted.
- Margaret enters into the fray now, and explains the impulse that she and her sister felt to help him – it has to do with the connection they felt with him last week, when he talked about his walk and his struggle against the dullness of life.
- Leonard responds huffily that they were pressing him for information and storms out. Helen goes to try and talk sense into him.
- Margaret is left with the Wilcoxes, who agree that she was splendid. She explains that he was the friend of theirs who works at the Porphyrion and jokingly blames Mr. Wilcox for the row, since it was his advice in the first place.
- Margaret blames herself and Helen for the fight, but the Wilcoxes think she's being too generous. They think Leonard is simply not of their "kind" – even Margaret agrees that he's not a gentleman, and that he suspected that they were taking advantage of him.
- She tries to make them understand what's interesting and likable about Leonard – his ambitions to escape humdrum everyday life. Mr. Wilcox, the voice of practical reason, gently shoots down all of Margaret's idealistic views.
- Mr. Wilcox and Evie assume that Leonard is cheating on his wife, and that he's fundamentally "naughty" and untruthful. Margaret holds out in her belief that he's honest in his desires to find something better, and that it makes him a "real man."
- Margaret goes to find out what Helen's doing; apparently, Leonard left a while ago. Margaret brings her sister back to the Wilcoxes, and they pretend that everything's OK. The puppies are a good distraction.
- As the Wilcoxes leave, Mr. Wilcox comments that he's worried about the Schlegels – they

shouldn't be left on their own.

- Evie admits that she likes Helen, but not Margaret. She's clearly not a kindred spirit; she is healthy, athletic, and attractive, but not a very poetic soul. A few days later, she suddenly but unromantically gets engaged.

Chapter 17

- Margaret is still worried about the housing problem – what will she do with her siblings and all of their things next September when they're kicked out of Wickham Place? Losing the house they grew up in is like losing a kind of spiritual balance.
- The siblings are due to visit Aunt Juley in Swanage, and Margaret really wants to fix the situation before they leave. But London doesn't seem to have anything to offer.
- One day, Evie invites Margaret to dine at Simpson's, a famously traditional restaurant that Margaret had jokingly complained about never having been to. Margaret's a little confused as to why Evie would ask *her*, instead of Helen, but she goes in good faith, thinking that they'll get to know each other better.
- Evie and her fiancé, Percy Cahill, are waiting for her at the restaurant. Margaret immediately feels patronized by them and feels like an old maid.
- Lo and behold, it's not just the three of them – Mr. Wilcox also turns up for lunch. He and Margaret fall into a conversation as Evie and Percy chat lovingly to each other. We learn that Mr. Wilcox used to have business in the East (Greece and Cyprus), and we wonder what he used to get up to there.
- Margaret enlists Mr. Wilcox's help in finding a house, to no avail.
- During lunch, Margaret observes a kind of English society – imperialist, capitalist, and masculine – that is totally unlike that which she's familiar with. Mr. Wilcox himself is extremely domineering, and takes a firm hand with telling her what to order for lunch.
- The conversation turns to Margaret's crowd and her beliefs. She jokes that Mr. Wilcox should come and have lunch with her at her friend Eustace Miles's, where the conversation is all about health food and auras. They chat a bit about spirituality, and he confirms – with some concern – that she doesn't actually believe in auras and astral planes.
- Margaret turns the conversation to Howards End, as she always seems to do. She asks if Mr. Wilcox might be able to rent it to the Schlegels, but alas, it's impossible.
- They talk about Leonard as well, and Margaret is disturbed by how well Mr. Wilcox seems to understand her. Their views on money, though they come from different philosophies, seem to converge.
- After lunch, Margaret leaves the Wilcoxes. She suspects that lunch was Mr. Wilcox's plan all along, and wonders why he's seeking further intimacy with her.
- Margaret actually takes Mr. Wilcox (and Tibby, for propriety's sake) to lunch at Eustace Miles's.
- The Schlegels depart for Aunt Juley's, without having found a house.

Chapter 18

- At Aunt Juley's house, Margaret receives a letter from Mr. Wilcox, saying that he's leaving his house in London – would the Schlegels like to rent it? If she's interested, she should come back to London right away to look at it.
- Margaret wonders if this is actually a veiled attempt to get her to London so he can propose marriage.
- Margaret presents the option of the Wilcoxes' house to her family. They are uncertain and argumentative, as usual. Tibby still doesn't really *get* the Wilcoxes and their importance.
- Margaret bemoans the difficulties they're having, saying that their father, who moved from Germany, never had such petty troubles. Aunt Juley corrects her, saying that they can't remember how difficult it was for their parents to move into Wickham Place – houses, apparently, always cause trouble.
- Margaret ends up going to London by herself to look at the house. She's worried that she's being a crazy spinster for thinking about the potential marriage proposal.
- Mr. Wilcox meets her at the station, and she can immediately tell that something's up. He's super-sensitive today.
- Mr. Wilcox seems kind of peevish – he complains of being lonely because Evie is always out with her fiancé. Margaret off-handedly comments that she's also lonely, and he seizes upon this. We begin to think that she's not so crazy after all – maybe a proposal is coming her way?
- Margaret is impressed and a little put off by Mr. Wilcox's way of going through life without bothering to investigate the personal or private things that distract her so often.
- She likes him nonetheless, and even finds him attractive, in his way.
- The car is full of unspoken emotion – of some kind – and Margaret senses again that something's up with her companion.
- They arrive at the Wilcoxes' house on Ducie Street, and go through the whole thing; Margaret wants to look over it before she can report back to Tibby and Helen.
- The house exudes an air of masculine power – and colonial, capitalist power. Margaret loves it.
- Finally, after they're done with the house, Mr. Wilcox does as expected: he pops the question. It's truly unromantic.
- All the same, Margaret is suddenly, amazingly happy. Overwhelmingly so. But she reins in her emotions and tells Mr. Wilcox that she will answer him by letter.
- Margaret goes home to Wickham Place and thinks over her proposal. She's been asked to marry men before, but none of them have ever had a chance. It seems that Margaret might actually be.. *in love*.
- She hasn't made up her mind, but it seems to us like she's going to accept. She has a rather odd attitude towards him – she doesn't want to push him to be emotional or overwhelm him with her emotions, since he's old and set in his ways.
- Margaret feels the friendly presence of Mrs. Wilcox, her predecessor, who seems to

approve. Creepy.

Chapter 19

- The narrator waxes lyrical about the beauties of the English countryside for a little while. The reason, we learn, is that Frieda is visiting the Schlegels and Aunt Juley at Swanage, but she doesn't admire the scene as fervently as Aunt Juley would like.
- Frieda and Aunt Juley have a silly almost-argument about the virtues of German salt marshes versus English lakes – this is clearly a national matter.
- The party observes a train coming towards them, and Helen wonders if Margaret is on it. They wonder about the Wilcoxes' house – will it do for the Schlegels?
- They have a little laugh over the Paul/Helen incident, and Helen declares that it doesn't matter anymore, as long as the Ducie Street house is nice.
- Helen wishes absently that they might have Howards End, since it's such a nice house.
- They discuss what Helen calls the "Great Wilcox Peril" of two summers ago as they wait for Tibby and Margaret to join them for tea on the hillside. Frieda makes a comment on the nature of love and emotional truth that reveals – to Helen and to the narrator – the essential difference between Germans and the English: the Germans are interested in Truth, while the English are interested in respectability. Or so it seems.
- Margaret and Tibby approach in a pony cart, and Helen, who can't wait to hear the news, wants to know if she got them a house.
- Margaret wearily says no, and explains quietly to Helen that she's had a marriage proposal from Mr. Wilcox.
- Helen is amused – then distinctly unamused when she realizes that Margaret is having feelings for her suitor.
- Helen throws a fit, telling Margaret that she mustn't marry Mr. Wilcox. Margaret thinks she's being a bit unreasonable.
- Helen can't explain exactly why she is so upset. Both sisters take a minute to calm down. Margaret explains how it happened. She feels sure that he loves her, and that she has started to love him.
- Helen tries to explain, in turn, her dislike for Mr. Wilcox, which began when she saw Paul frightened by his father – the Wilcoxes deal too much in the outside world of respectability and doing the proper thing, not the thing that one *feels* is right.
- Margaret has no romantic illusions about her relationship; she knows that it will be prose, not poetry, as she phrases it. But she's OK with this – the important thing is that Mr. Wilcox is a good man, and a *real* man.
- Margaret is determined not to let her marriage take over her whole life, and expects that he and she will continue to be independent characters.
- She respects the Wilcoxes for what they've done – ancestrally, in a weird sense. They're the kind of people that make England what it is, and she values that. Helen tries to dismiss that impulse, but Margaret will have none of it.

- Again, the narrator wonders poetically what makes England *England* – the land itself is somehow alive and animated by something.

Chapter 20

- Margaret ponders the nature of love in relation to its legal validation, Matrimony. It's an odd relationship. She agrees to marry him, and their relationship, which is founded on "good humor" progresses to a new level.
- Mr. Wilcox shows up at Swanage the next day with a ring for Margaret. He comes over for dinner, and they go on a walk alone afterwards. Margaret is surprised that love is not the way it's portrayed in books.
- They go over the progress of their relationship from the day on the Chelsea Embankment (Chapter 15, if you want to look back) to the present. Only ten days have passed, but everything is different now.
- Mr. Wilcox has already had a chat with Tibby about the marriage (and about a currant farm he owns in Greece – Tibby is interested in Greece for academic reasons, not business ones). Margaret is delighted about the idea of visiting the farm, but since there are no hotels there, Mr. Wilcox vetoes that idea – he thinks ladies should always travel like *ladies*, unlike Helen and Margaret's past lives of gallivanting around.
- Mr. Wilcox hasn't yet talked to Helen about the marriage, and Margaret presses him to.
- They also have to talk about some practical matters pertaining to money – Mr. Wilcox wants to make sure that all of his children get their fair share of the family fortune, but he also wants to be fair to Margaret.
- Margaret is totally up front about her financial situation (she has plenty of money), and Mr. Wilcox is a little taken aback by it. Margaret brushes it off, saying that he's to decide how much to give to each to each of his children, bearing in mind that she has her own fortune.
- They move on to practical arrangements about their living situation – where will they live? Margaret says they should keep the Ducie Street house, but now, all of a sudden (since he's not trying to get her to rent it), Mr. Wilcox has all kinds of problems with it. Margaret is amused.
- The narrator observes that Mr. Wilcox and Margaret are both strong-willed, and that their mutual strength ensures that they will be happy.
- Mr. Wilcox walks Margaret back to Aunt Juley's house, and – rather unexpectedly – they have their first kiss, and he flees the house. Margaret is unimpressed, and even displeased by it.

Chapter 21

- Charles and Dolly are in a fight – or rather, Charles is berating Dolly for the situation the Wilcoxes are in. He blames her not only for Evie's coming marriage to Percy, but also for Mr. Wilcox's marriage to Margaret.
- Charles assumes that Margaret was just out to get Howards End, and fatalistically thinks that she's accomplished her goal.
- Dolly calms him down, and calms down the baby, who's upset by this parental strife. Charles subsides, muttering something about keeping an eye on "these Schlegels."

Chapter 22

- Margaret feels particularly loving towards Mr. Wilcox the next day. She sees that he's not connected to his own feelings, and is even ashamed of them, and she hopes to cure him of that.
- Margaret's mantra is simple: "only connect" (hint: this is the most important catch-phrase of the novel…if you only remember one thing about *Howards End*, make it this!). She wants for people to be able to join the disparate parts of their own souls, and thus to be able to connect to other humans, as well.
- However, there's something in Mr. Wilcox that resists this commandment; he just doesn't notice things about other people. He focuses instead on "concentrating" and getting things to work out his way, despite the feelings of others. For example, he doesn't notice that the other Schlegels don't like him.
- Helen shows up, and they talk about a letter she's had from Leonard Bast, saying that he left the Porphyrion, following Mr. Wilcox's advice. In passing, Mr. Wilcox mentions offhandedly that the Porphyrion's not a bad business after all.
- Margaret is mortified: what does he mean, not a bad business? Didn't he just tell them a few weeks ago that it was going to crash?
- Mr. Wilcox goes about his business greeting Aunt Juley and Frieda, but Helen and Margaret are upset.
- Margaret asks about the Porphyrion once she gets Mr. Wilcox off on his own – he tells her that the new bank he has a job at is a safe bet, and she feels better.
- The conversation shifts to the matter of Howards End; the guy leasing it has to go abroad, and wants to sublet it. Mr. Wilcox isn't cool with this, and is worried that the house might be damaged. He suggests that he and Margaret go and take a look at the house, and also visit Charles and Dolly.
- Margaret agrees, but can't cut short her visit with Aunt Juley. Mr. Wilcox high-handedly says that he'll take care of Aunt Juley.
- Margaret *does* really want to see Howards End. She mentions the pigs' teeth in the wych elm that Mrs. Wilcox told her about – Mr. Wilcox dismisses this as a fairytale.
- He goes off to talk to Aunt Juley, and Helen stops him en route to confront him about the

Porphyrion.

- Helen is angry: she can't believe that Mr. Wilcox warned them off the Porphyrion, but it's good after all. It turns out that Leonard's new job has a much lower salary, and, acting upon Mr. Wilcox's advice, he's gone down in the world.
- Helen and Mr. Wilcox just don't understand each other; she doesn't get that business is a gamble, and he doesn't get why she's upset about Leonard.
- Mr. Wilcox continues to offend Helen by telling her not to worry about the poor – there's nothing she can do directly to help them.
- Helen is upset, not just by Mr. Wilcox himself, but by all that he represents. She's also clearly upset by her own position as an old maid. She flees Margaret and goes into the house.
- Aunt Juley comes up, also upset, because Mr. Wilcox has broken the news that they're leaving early. Margaret feels a surge of love for her fiancé, and, even though she doesn't understand him fully, it doesn't bother her.

Chapter 23

- Margaret and Helen have something of an odd argument over Margaret's decision to marry Mr. Wilcox. Helen gives in and tells her sister to go ahead and marry him, but not to expect her to like him. Rather, she's determined to keep disliking him (and not hide it), and to fully go about things her own way from now on.
- Helen at least grants that she will be civil to Mr. Wilcox in public, if Margaret will do the same with *her* friends.
- Everything between the two sisters themselves is fine; Margaret is reassured that Helen will still love her, at least. She returns to London to meet Henry (Mr. Wilcox).
- The next morning, she shows up at his office (the Imperial and West African Rubber Company). She's met by Charles, who, despite his indignation, is polite to her. He talks down Howards End, no doubt with the intention of putting Margaret off it.
- Mr. Wilcox shows up as they're discussing the bad behavior of their lessor, Mr. Bryce, who's already started advertising for a subletter, even though they said not to. He put up a notice on the house, but Charles tore it down.
- Mr. Wilcox and Margaret leave Charles at work and drive down to Hilton. The scenery is pretty, and presently, they arrive at the village.
- Dolly meets them at their house, and offers them lunch, during which the conversation is pleasant and mocking, and Margaret meets her future step-grandchildren.
- After lunch, they go to Howards End, and Margaret finally gets to see the house for the first time. Mr. Wilcox has forgotten the key, so he goes back to grab it, leaving Margaret on her own.
- She first sees the trees and the garden, which she finds perfectly beautiful. She discovers that the house is actually open, and goes in. It's dirty and unkempt, but she still finds it all beautiful.

- Margaret roams the house, thinking of the value of space and empire, and is interrupted by the appearance of a mysterious old woman, who simply says that Margaret reminded her of Ruth Wilcox. The old woman walks out into the rain, leaving Margaret mystified.

Chapter 24

- Mr. Wilcox relates the tale of Margaret's odd encounter to Dolly over tea. The old woman is apparently called Miss Avery, and Mr. Wilcox thinks she's just a silly old maid.
- Dolly asks if Margaret thought Miss Avery was a "spook" (Dolly is not the most spiritually informed of girls) and, though Margaret says that she wasn't frightened, Mr. Wilcox thinks that she was.
- Mr. Wilcox and Dolly have a dismissive attitude towards Miss Avery, who they class as "uneducated." Mr. Wilcox complains about women like her; he doesn't like her at all, but Margaret thinks she might.
- Dolly goes off on a tangent about Miss Avery's history with the family. Apparently, the first Mrs. Wilcox's brother, Tom Howard, proposed to her (which would have made her Charles and Evie's aunt), but she said no, and he died soon after.
- Mr. Wilcox makes their excuses, and says that they've got to leave. Margaret smiles to herself, noting that the Wilcoxes can't possibly coexist near each other – they all have competitive colonial instincts.
- Crane, the chauffeur, brings the car round, and they return to London.
- Margaret, home alone at Wickham Place, thinks over the day she had. Mr. Wilcox showed her all around Howards End, telling her about the improvements he'd made on it, and, at the end of the day, they discovered that she was right about the pigs' teeth in the wych elm – Mr. Wilcox is shocked.

Chapter 25

- Evie hears about Mr. Wilcox's engagement while she's playing tennis, and it totally throws her game off. She, Charles, and Dolly are all upset about their new stepmother, and in order to cope, Evie moves her own wedding up by a month, to August.
- Margaret, it turns out, is expected to participate actively in Evie's wedding, and to meet all of Mr. Wilcox's friends and associates. This is not exciting to her – she loves Henry, but hates all of his friends. He doesn't seem to have any feelings himself for any of these people, but instead, has a sense of whether they're useful or not.
- Evie decides to get married at the house at Oniton Grange, in Shropshire. Mr. Wilcox isn't too fond of the house, and intends to lease it out once Evie is married.
- Margaret, however, thinks of it as her future home, and decides to make the best impression possible there.

- There aren't many people at the wedding, considering that Paul can't make it, Dolly has to stay home and Tibby and Helen both refused to come. Margaret thinks forward rather wearily to her own wedding.
- The group of guests coming from London travel together on the train, and when they get a rest stop at Shrewsbury before driving to Oniton, Margaret takes the opportunity to do some sightseeing. She overhears Charles complaining about how the women are making them late. Finally, they get on the road, and they chat about politics on the way.
- Just before they arrive at the Grange, one of the cars hits a dog. Charles doesn't even stop – he doesn't care. Margaret, however, is horribly upset, and demands that they stop and go back. She gets so upset that she actually hurls herself out of the car.
- It turns out that it was a cat, not a dog, and the little girl who owned it was understandably very upset.
- When they get to the Grange, Margaret offers a little playful explanation to Henry, and when she goes away to change, Charles tells his father all about the incident. They agree that it was probably just "nerves."
- Charles is upset – he can't stand any of the Schlegels, and he can't believe how crazy Margaret is.
- Charles clearly has a chip on his shoulder about everything, and he feels quite put upon as he observes the wedding guests coming and going. He clearly really hates Margaret.
- Secretly watched by her future son-in-law, Margaret wanders around the grounds, enchanted by the scenery. He's sure that she's up to trouble.

Chapter 26

- The next morning, Margaret observes as the men of the party go for a swim, and is then summoned up to Evie's room to view the wedding dress.
- The women are all practically hysterical over the dress – they're ecstatically screaming and fussing over Evie, and are generally acting like stereotypical silly women.
- After breakfast, Margaret and Mr. Wilcox chat about the practicalities of the wedding. Margaret seems to really love him, albeit in a somewhat odd way. They go together through the house, looking for Burton, the butler.
- Margaret is trying to get used to Oniton, and to figure out the workings of the house.
- The wedding happens uneventfully, and everyone is pleased by everything. Evie and Percy leave on their honeymoon, and Margaret and Mr. Wilcox talk about their own wedding. Margaret doesn't want to talk about where they'll have their wedding; instead, she's interested in the evening, and looking out at Oniton.
- Some unexpected visitors show up: it's Helen, with the Basts in tow. She's furious, and she tells Margaret angrily that Leonard and Jacky are "starving," and that it's their fault.
- Margaret and Helen get into a fight: Margaret is justifiably angry that Helen has disrupted the wedding, and that she's embarrassed her sister in front of her new friends and family.
- Margaret confronts the Basts. Jacky is confused by what's going on, and Leonard is

embarrassed.

- Helen explains her so-called logical reasons for this visit. She's convinced that it's the Schlegels' fault, and Mr. Wilcox's, for telling Leonard to leave the Porphyrion, and she wants Mr. Wilcox to fix the situation somehow.
- Margaret basically says that there's no hope – in her opinion, it's not anyone's fault, and there's nothing to be done. She offers to put the Basts up at the local hotel, and says that they can pay her back later.
- Leonard gets upset at this, saying that he'll never find another job, and that he and Jacky are destined for poverty – in the world they live in, if a lower-class man loses his job, he's lost for life. We're reminded again of the difference that being born with money makes.
- Margaret doesn't know how to respond to this; she invites the Basts to eat something at the wedding party while she figures things out.
- Margaret and Helen have a quick conference – the older sister convinces the younger to take the Basts to the hotel, and says that she will talk to Mr. Wilcox about it in her own way.
- Margaret goes back to Mr. Wilcox, who wants to know what's up. She explains that Helen's here, and he thinks that she's there for Evie's wedding. Margaret says that she's sent them off to the hotel, and that she'll explain later.
- This just makes Mr. Wilcox more curious, so Margaret explains right away about the Basts and their situation.
- Mr. Wilcox says that he'll do what he can for Leonard, but can't guarantee anything – and furthermore, in the future, he can't always have room for her protégés.
- Margaret is happy; as usual, she admires men and their capability. Despite Henry's flaws, she has confidence in him.
- Henry and Margaret stumble upon Jacky, and Margaret is disturbed by her – she feels like the woman represents a kind of infringement upon the world that she knows, even though Jacky isn't at all malicious. She's eating wedding cake and is obviously drunk.
- Mr. Wilcox sternly tries to send Jacky away – but she recognizes him, and calls him "Hen." They obviously know each other – but how?
- Margaret, trying to be discreet, tells Mr. Wilcox in French that Mr. Bast isn't at all like his wife.
- Jacky keeps trying to talk to Mr. Wilcox, and tells him that she loves him. Margaret is totally confused, for good reason.
- Mr. Wilcox is sure that this is a set-up, and that Margaret and Helen have been plotting against him. He admits to having had "a man's past," and says that Margaret is set free from their engagement. She's still confused and horrified.
- Margaret knows that life can be darker than she thinks…but she can't quite make herself comprehend the situation.
- Colonel Fussell comes along and Margaret and Henry pretend that everything's OK. As soon as he goes away, though, they have a confrontation. Margaret asks if Jacky was Henry's mistress: she was, ten years ago. Margaret goes away, deciding that the affair was the last Mrs. Wilcox's problem, not hers.

Chapter 27

- Helen begins to doubt herself – what's she doing, anyway? She figures that it'll all work out in the long run.
- Helen strives to explain Mr. Wilcox to Leonard after they put the drunk Jacky to bed. She tells him that she believes in "personal responsibility," meaning that she thinks everyone should think of themselves in depth and come to a level of personal understanding.
- The world, according to Helen, is divided into people who have this sense of responsibility and self (like Leonard, Helen, and Margaret), and those who don't – like Mr. Wilcox, and other powerful men of his ilk.
- Leonard has rather complicated feelings about Helen – he feels somewhat proprietary of her, and is beginning to think that he doesn't like her sister (he wonders if Helen herself does).
- Unbeknownst to Helen, Leonard already knows about Mr. Wilcox's relationship to Jacky, but doesn't want Helen to find out.
- Helen asks about Jacky, which makes Leonard uncomfortable. The couple has been married for three years, and it clearly hasn't been a good marriage. Leonard's family has cut him off entirely because of it.
- Helen, never one for discretion, asks about his family (his immediate family members are all lower-middle class and his grandparents were actually laborers – though Leonard is embarrassed, Helen doesn't look down on him). Helen asks why they don't approve of Jacky, and she figures out the truth – Jacky was a prostitute.
- Leonard tries to get Helen to stop worrying about his problems, and tells her that he'll just settle down to ordinary life after they get back to London. Helen is troubled by this – after all, he's the man that used to walk at night and yearn for something more.
- Leonard himself dismisses books, and says that he's learned not to have so many fantasies; in order to be a dreamer, one also has to be rich.
- Helen explains that in her philosophy, things like money and practicality are the opposite of real life – and men like Mr. Wilcox don't really understand capital-L Life.
- Leonard is confused by all of this; he wants to engage at this higher level, but he's still occupied by the very real troubles of his life. Where will he get a job? What will he do? Talk can only go so far.
- Helen keeps talking about death, trying to explain that understanding the idea of it puts everything in perspective and teaches people to truly value love and life. Her generalizations are poetic, but, we suspect, extremely naïve.
- A letter for Helen (from Margaret) arrives, as well as a note for Leonard.

Chapter 28

- Margaret spends hours thinking over everything that's happened, then writes a bunch of letters.

- The first is to Henry; she writes it instinctively, saying that everything will be fine between them, then edits it according to his taste. He's clearly changed her.
- Margaret then reevaluates, and wonders if she really *can* deal with the fact that Mr. Wilcox had an affair with Jacky. She tears up the letter she just wrote.
- Next, she writes a brief note to Leonard, saying that Mr. Wilcox can't get him a job.
- She also writes a letter to Helen, telling her that they found Jacky drunk, and that the Basts are not worth her while – she should ditch them, and come to stay with the Wilcoxes at the house.
- Margaret feels like she's handling the matters in a practical fashion. She delivers the letters to the hotel herself, and sees Helen watching her through the window.
- She goes to inform Henry of what she's done, telling him that Helen is coming to spend the night.
- They act like nothing's happened, but obviously, something important has.
- Margaret tries to decide if she can stay with Henry or not. She goes back and forth between anger and pity – and ultimately decides to forgive him.

Chapter 29

- The next morning, Margaret confronts Mr. Wilcox. She tells him it doesn't make any difference to her, and he gets angry at this – he thinks that she's not acting like a real woman, and that she should be upset.
- Henry tries to push Margaret away, saying that he's not worthy of her love. He believes in the distinct difference between men and women, and the worlds they live in.
- Margaret inquires about Helen, only to find that she didn't show up last night. She's worried that Helen will find out the truth about Henry and Jacky and spread the story. Mr. Wilcox thinks it's no use to try and stop it from getting out.
- Henry gives in to emotion and tells Margaret the story of his relationship with Jacky. Ten years ago, they met in Cyprus – and the rest is history. Margaret makes him feel better by telling him that she's already forgiven him.
- Margaret goes to the hotel to try and rustle up her sister. When she returns, Mr. Wilcox is recovered from his bout with emotion, and is his old, businesslike self.
- Margaret has some bad news – the Basts and Helen have all gone from the hotel, with no word about their whereabouts.
- Margaret and Henry take a walk around the garden. Henry makes her promise never to mention Jacky again; he's worried that they might blackmail him, and tells his fiancée that he'll take care of the situation.
- When they get back to the house, Mr. Wilcox basically puts the matter out of his mind – Margaret has forgiven him, and his children must never hear about it. That's all that matters.
- Margaret herself is worried about Leonard and, like Helen, feels responsible for his troubles. That being said, though, she doesn't want to do anything about it; she's made

up her mind to continue loving Mr. Wilcox, and to become part of his world.

Chapter 30

- Tibby lives in his own world at Oxford, and he clearly doesn't like to be troubled by the lives of others. He's a classic academic, and though he's not a particularly bad person, he never descends from his ivory tower. At present, he's learning Chinese, and it's his principal pastime.
- Helen turns up one day, after warning Tibby of her arrival with a telegram. She tells him about her adventure in Oniton, and tells him that she's not going back home to Wickham Place.
- Tibby is more concerned with lunch than with his sister's troubles.
- Helen goes on, saying that he's to tell Margaret that she just wants to be alone – she's going to Germany. As for the house, her siblings can do what they like about it.
- Tibby asks if something happened at Evie's wedding, and Helen starts to cry. He doesn't want her to ruin his lunch, so he goes right on eating.
- Helen pulls herself together, and brings up Mr. Wilcox, hinting ominously that he's done something terrible and ruined lives. She mentions the Basts, and Tibby is exasperated.
- Tibby assumes correctly that this means that Mr. Wilcox has had a mistress, and Helen launches into an attack on Mr. Wilcox's behavior towards the Basts. She thinks it's his fault that they're paupers. She then explains the Leonard situation.
- Tibby admits that it's a very unfortunate series of events. Helen wants him to decide what to do about this knowledge about Mr. Wilcox, but Tibby has no opinion on what to do about Margaret's involvement in all of this. He prefers to deal with people in books, not in person.
- Helen has given up on stopping Margaret's marriage, but now she's worried about compensating the Basts for Mr. Wilcox's wrongs. She wants to give them five thousand pounds.
- Tibby is taken aback, but his sister is determined to give them this huge sum, and she puts him in charge of doling it out.
- Tibby walks his sister to the train station, and he is quite affected by her distress – at least, until he gets distracted by a statue on his way home.
- The next day, Margaret and Tibby meet. She asks if Helen was upset about a rumor about Henry, and Tibby, thankful to be relieved of his duties, says yes.
- He takes care of the second task Helen set to him by sending a check for the Basts, but it's returned with a civil note that says the money is not needed. Helen is upset, and insists that Tibby go back and force the money upon the Basts.
- However, the Basts are nowhere to be found – they were evicted, and nobody knows where they went.
- Helen, dismayed, isn't sure what to do with her money. She takes it out of her stocks, but, not knowing what to do, ends up reinvesting it and becoming even richer than before.

Chapter 31

- It's moving time at Wickham Place. The Schlegels' furniture is mostly moved to Howards End; the guy leasing the house actually died abroad, so it's empty until someone else comes along to rent it.
- Right before the big move, Henry and Margaret are married quietly. There's no big wedding – Tibby gives Margaret away, and Aunt Juley organizes food and drink. The marriage goes off uneventfully.
- Henry and Margaret spend their honeymoon in the Alps. Margaret hopes to see her sister, who's still in Germany, but Helen evades her sister and brother-in-law.
- Margaret, thinking that Helen just doesn't want to see Mr. Wilcox, writes her a long, critical letter about how Helen shouldn't be so judgmental. Helen simply thanks her for her letter.
- Mr. Wilcox doesn't mind being apart from Helen, since she reminds him of his shameful behavior in the past (with Jacky, and with another affair in his youth). He grows fonder and fonder of Margaret, who seems to be becoming more submissive and feminine in her married state. He enjoys her intellect, but in a condescending way – he always has to win an argument.
- One real problem with the marriage, however, is where they're going to live. Henry has leased Oniton Grange out, which annoys Margaret, who'd assumed that they'd live there. They end up moving to the Ducie Street house for the winter.
- Margaret and Henry move to Ducie Street and properly settle into married life. Margaret loses touch with her old friends and old life, and begins to lose track of her liberal agendas and intellectual concerns. We're informed that she's moved from "words to things" – is this a good thing?

Chapter 32

- The Wilcoxes decide to build a new house in Sussex, and one day, as Margaret is examining the plans, Dolly bursts in.
- Dolly has big news, but she's distracted for a bit as she relates the local gossip to Margaret. They discuss the new house, then Helen, then Charles and Dolly's financial situation (which isn't great).
- Finally, Dolly remembers what she came to talk about: Miss Avery, the old lady who takes care of Howards End, has started unpacking all of the Schlegels' belongings and laying them out in the house, even their books.
- At the mention of books, Margaret is in an uproar – some of them are Tibby's, and are valuable. She's justifiably upset at Miss Avery, who has no right to open up all of their things.
- Dolly thinks Miss Avery's just crazy, and says that she hates all of the Wilcoxes since

Evie's wedding. Apparently, she bought Evie a wedding present (a necklace) that everyone thought was too expensive to accept, and when Evie returned it, she got terribly upset and threw it into the pond.

- Henry, apparently, knew about Miss Avery's battiness, but still wanted her to look after Howards End; he has infinite patience for people who are good at what they do.
- After asking Henry's permission, Margaret writes a note to Miss Avery, asking her not to touch any of her things. She goes to Howards End herself to sort out the unpacked books situation and store them elsewhere. Though Tibby promises to go, he unsurprisingly backs out in the end, leaving his sister to visit the house alone.

Chapter 33

- It's a beautiful day in Hilton, and the narrator ominously tells us that it's the last happy day Margaret will have for a while. She walks through the village, and as she does, the narrator muses about England and Englishness (we should be used to this by now), wondering why England doesn't have a national mythology.
- Margaret gets to the Avery farm, where she stops to pick up the keys to Howards End. She's met by Miss Avery's young niece, who seems to hold her in great respect. Since Miss Avery is at Howards End (apparently she spends a lot of time there), the young lady insists on walking Margaret to the house.
- Miss Avery is indeed at Howards End, and she's locked herself in. She sends her embarrassed niece, Madge, away, but lets Margaret into the house.
- Miss Avery politely and sanely invites Margaret in, and she's alarmed to see that all of the furnishings of the house are her own. Miss Avery has even hung up the Schlegels' father's sword, which seems like rather an odd choice.
- Margaret tries to explain that the cases were meant to stay packed up, and that they're not moving into the house.
- Miss Avery simply states that the house has been empty for too long, and Margaret does her best to reason with the stubborn old lady.
- There's some confusion about the "Mrs. Wilcoxes" that Miss Avery keeps referring to – is she referring to Ruth or Margaret? One thing is clear: she thinks that the house belongs to Mrs. Wilcox, whichever one.
- Miss Avery walks Margaret through the house, which is almost completely furnished with the Schlegel belongings. Margaret protests that she and Mr. Wilcox aren't going to live at Howards End, but Miss Avery is not to be dissuaded – she says ominously that Margaret doesn't think she'll ever live at Howards End, but she will. She oddly states that Margaret has been living there for the last ten minutes. Seriously weird.
- Miss Avery mocks the Wilcoxes for their hay fever – they're unfit to live in the country. She admits that Wilcoxes are better than nothing, but she clearly has real disdain for them.
- For Ruth Wilcox and her family, the Howards, however, Miss Avery has great affection and respect. She thinks that Ruth shouldn't ever have married Henry; instead, she says, her

old friend should have married "a real soldier," a statement that obliquely criticizes Mr. Wilcox.

- Margaret tells Miss Avery once more that they're not moving in to Howards End, then makes her excuses and goes back to London, where Mr. Wilcox has some suggestions about what to do with the furniture.
- Before she can sort it all out, though, she has an unfortunate surprise.

Chapter 34

- Sadly, poor Aunt Juley is in bad health – this isn't actually entirely a surprise, but it's unfortunate nonetheless. She has pneumonia, and Tibby and Margaret go to Swanage to look after her. They send for Helen.
- Aunt Juley is in a bad state, and Margaret worries that she will die.
- Helen says she can only come to see Aunt Juley, and must return as soon as she's better – she can't stay and hang out in England, for some reason.
- Aunt Juley, thankfully, doesn't actually die. Nobody can figure out why Helen didn't come back when her aunt was at risk. It's a mystery.
- Margaret doesn't want to admit it, but she's really worried about Helen. It seems that Helen's dislike for Henry is the cause of her staying away. Margaret worries that this hatred of the Wilcoxes has driven her a little batty.
- Margaret grows more and more worried, as all humans do – once we get a thought in our heads, it's impossible not to let it get out of hand.
- Helen sends a letter saying that she'll be in London soon, but that she will only come to Swanage if Aunt Juley is absolutely in dire condition. She wants to know where their stuff is so she can reclaim some of her books. The letter is affectionate, but totally weird.
- Margaret wants to lie and tell Helen that Aunt Juley really needs her, but she ends up telling the truth. Tibby, who's grown up a bit and has become rather a pleasant but cold human being (against all odds), thinks she's done the right thing. Furthermore, he thinks Margaret should tell Mr. Wilcox, but she doesn't want to.
- Margaret tries to get Helen to meet with her at their bank, but Helen doesn't show up. Margaret feels desperate, and gives in and asks Henry what to do.
- Mr. Wilcox at first just says it's just like Helen to act all crazy and lead them on a wild goose chase, but Margaret is dissatisfied by this answer. Tibby steps in to tell Mr. Wilcox that they're worried that Helen has gone insane. This alarms Charles.
- Tibby calmly relates the facts: Helen is evading her siblings at every turn, but refuses to tell them why. Margaret emphasizes the fact that they don't think Helen is well – she may not be totally mad, but she's definitely not OK.
- This gets Mr. Wilcox's attention. Sick people are a different matter; he immediately takes an interest and comes up with a devious plan to trick Helen into coming to Howards End under the pretense of getting her books, where Henry and Margaret will ambush her.
- Margaret resists, but is won over by Tibby and Henry, who both think it's the right thing to

do.

- Charles is the only one who doesn't agree, as he doesn't want Howards End involved.
- Margaret also still has misgivings, but she does as Mr. Wilcox says. The meeting is planned for Monday at 3.
- Charles still has a very bad feeling about all of this. So do we.

Chapter 35

- The fatal day arrives, and we find Mr. Wilcox and Margaret in Hilton with Dolly. Margaret is anxious, and Mr. Wilcox wants to go spring on Helen without her.
- Margaret runs to the washroom to gather herself, and Mr. Wilcox sneaks out without her, telling Dolly to make an excuse.
- The car starts on its way, but Dolly and Charles's little boy accidentally sits in the middle of the driveway, causing the chauffeur to swerve off course. Dolly screams, and Margaret comes running out.
- Margaret confronts Henry about his attempt to cut her out of the plan, and he apologizes. The apology is accepted, and they embark again.
- The car stops to pick up the doctor, and Henry emphasizes how important it is not to scare Helen. The doctor and Henry discuss Helen's case dispassionately, and Margaret is infuriated by the way they're busily labeling her character, as though she's not even human.
- Margaret is determined to be on Helen's side, since it's obvious that nobody else is.
- Helen is innocently waiting on the porch at Howards End. Margaret runs out of the car before Henry can stop her, and rushes to her sister. She discovers immediately why Helen has been avoiding everyone – she's pregnant.
- In a rush, Margaret unlocks the door and pushes Helen into the house, then calls out to Mr. Wilcox that everything is OK.

Chapter 36

- Henry tries to interfere, since Margaret looks so upset, but she won't let him into the house. She openly disobeys him for the first time, and feels like this is a fight of women against men.
- The doctor then tries to intervene, saying that Helen might be having a nervous breakdown.
- Margaret turns away both of them, saying that she and Helen don't need them – her sister still has a long while before the baby's due.
- Margaret appeals to Henry, saying that it's all about love – she cares for Helen, and neither of them do.

- The men give in and depart; Henry is confused by all of this, and Margaret tells him she will meet him at Charles and Dolly's.
- Margaret goes back into the house, where she confronts Helen.

Chapter 37

- Margaret tries to kiss Helen, but her sister resists, basically accusing her of dishonestly tricking her into coming to Howards End. She is justifiably annoyed, and Margaret admits that she shouldn't have done it.
- Helen is businesslike, and describes her situation in full: the baby's due in June, and she is never going to return to England, since English people will never forgive her for her transgression. She intends to stay in Munich with Monica, a feminist Italian journalist that she's befriended.
- Margaret imagines what Monica's like – the kind of "crude feminist" that the Schlegels used to make fun of.
- Helen emphasizes the fact that she can't live in England anymore.
- The talk turns to Howards End – they comment on how alive it feels with all of their things unpacked. Margaret is distracted for a short while, but gets to the point – she wants to know why Helen can't just come back. Is it because she hates Henry?
- Helen admits that it's not Henry's fault, but society's. There's no way she, with her illegitimate child, can fit into English society again. Margaret can't disagree with this.
- Margaret and Helen feel strangely and irrevocably separated – by what? By society, maybe, or the baby, or something else.
- Helen prepares to leave, and the sisters part amicably. As Helen's on her way out, though, a card arrives from Mr. Wilcox, instructing her to keep Helen around and put her up in a hotel.
- Helen, however, is suddenly not inclined to leave right away. She takes a look around the house, and can't believe how well all of their things fit there – as though they belong there.
- The door bell rings. The idea that the Wilcoxes might be there to interrupt suddenly brings the sisters together again, and they rediscover their connection.
- It's not the Wilcoxes, though – it's a little boy, Tom, who's come with some milk. He was sent by Miss Avery, who seems to think that the sisters will be staying at Howards End.
- Tom goes away, and Margaret and Helen try to figure out what is so special about Howards End – it seems to make everything feel all right again.
- Helen has an idea – why don't they spend the night at Howards End, before she leaves for Germany?
- Margaret resists, knowing that Charles and Henry won't agree to it. But Helen insists – she feels a kind of kinship with the house.
- Helen reiterates the difference between Schlegels and Wilcoxes – she and Margaret *know* about life in a way that Henry and Charles don't.
- Margaret agrees to the plan, and goes off to talk to her husband. She worries that Miss

Avery is watching, but she sees only little Tom.

Chapter 38

- Margaret returns to Charles and Dolly's house, and settles into a discussion with Henry about Helen. He tries immediately to take control, and treat her like an ignorant, submissive wife – but she'll have none of that.
- Margaret tries to jump straight in with her request about Howards End, but Henry's not done. He wants to know who Helen's "seducer" is, and Margaret doesn't know – she didn't even ask.
- Henry has tried to rally all of the menfolk; he called Charles to tell him about the situation, and Charles, in turn, is paying Tibby a visit. They intend to make Helen's lover marry her, or to otherwise punish him.
- Margaret gets to the point. She tells Henry that Helen's going to Munich tomorrow, but would like to sleep at Howards End that night. This is a more difficult question for him than it seems like it should be – he doesn't understand the impulse.
- Margaret tries to explain that Helen wants to be among their things, as a kind of end to her youth and innocence.
- Henry jumps to a negative conclusion – if Helen stays there one night, maybe she'll never leave.
- This offends Margaret, who's upset about the implication. Would it be so bad if Helen stayed?
- Margaret reveals that she wants to stay in Howards End with Helen, which upsets Henry even more. The two of them find themselves at an impasse.
- Margaret is at the end of her rope. She demands that Henry answer her plainly, and restates all of the facts – can't he forgive Helen for having a lover, since Margaret has forgiven him for Jacky? Can't they just spend one night in Howards End?
- Henry refuses, saying that he has to be respectful to his children and the first Mrs. Wilcox – Helen can't stay.
- Margaret, desperate, mentions Jacky again, then comes right out and accuses Mr. Wilcox of all of his crimes – cheating on his first wife, casting Jacky off (to ruin Leonard, in turn), not being responsible for Leonard's job. She tells him that he's done just the same thing that Helen's done (and more), but he just can't face up to it.
- Henry gathers his senses and flatly refuses once more, accusing Margaret of trying to blackmail him. He returns to the house; Margaret stays outside, fuming.

Chapter 39

- Charles meets with Tibby at the house at Ducie Street. The two of them have nothing at all in common, and their conversation is a travesty.
- Charles is determined to get rid of Helen, who he sees as nothing but a liability.
- Tibby, however, has the luxury of wealth and freedom, and he thinks that Helen should be able to do whatever she perceives to be right. His life of leisure has made him unsympathetic to the struggles of others.
- Charles tries to get Tibby riled up about Helen's pregnancy, and tries to get him to admit the identity of Helen's mystery man.
- Tibby, menaced by Charles, mentions that Helen had brought up the Basts before – but he says nothing else.
- Charles takes this to be an admission of guilt, and assumes that Tibby aided and abetted in Helen's affair with Leonard; disgusted, he storms out.

Chapter 40

- Helen finally opens up to Margaret about Leonard, but Margaret is confused by how Helen fell in love – with an idea, rather than with a man.
- The night is all about Helen coming clean and evaluating everything; she realizes that she'd blamed Mr. Wilcox for everything when she should have.
- Helen also feels guilty about the way in which her relationship with Leonard fell out – after the fact, she never wanted to see him again.
- Helen's clearly grown a lot; she says she now understands Margaret's marriage to Henry, and even if she never likes him, she'll always understand.
- Margaret says that only Mrs. Wilcox can and ever understood everyone – there was something magical about her that allowed her to see through everything.
- The sisters greet Miss Avery, and note that they are still like tourists at Howards End; they wonder if they will always be only tourists everywhere.
- Helen invites Margaret to join her in Germany – her sister is tempted, but doesn't know if she can bear to leave England.
- The two of them enjoy a moment of peace under the wych elm tree, and everything seems quiet and still. They embrace and say good night. Margaret wonders once again if everyone, even Leonard Bast, is a part of Mrs. Wilcox's mind.

Chapter 41

- Poor Leonard is not having a good time; he, unlike Helen, hasn't been able to intellectually

process their affair. He's full of remorse.

- Leonard never once imagines that it might be Helen's fault, or that they might at least share the blame. We, however, see that she is just as responsible as he was, or perhaps more – she loves things that are absolute, and Leonard's total destruction appealed to her.
- The morning after their tryst, Helen was gone. She left a note that meant to be kind, but broke Leonard's heart; he felt immediately terrified and guilty, as though he'd ruined her.
- The trip to Evie's wedding really destroyed the Basts financially. Helen, in her fit of passion, forgot to pay the hotel bill, and also ran off with their return train tickets. Despite all of her talk about being responsible, we see that she was really careless, selfish, and destructive.
- Leonard, desperate, was forced to ask his estranged family for money. He succeeds in wheedling some cash out of his two sisters and their husbands, but this just makes them hate each other more.
- The only things that keep Leonard alive are his sense of really *living*, even if it means suffering, and his affection for Jacky. He seems to view her as a kind of pathetic animal who needs care; this sense of duty keeps him going.
- One day, Leonard sees Margaret and Tibby from afar. He wants to come clean and tell them everything – he trusts Margaret, and decides that he must talk to her. He figures out where she lives, and stops by Ducie Street.
- Leonard finds out from the maid, who finds out from Tibby that Margaret is at Howards End, in Hilton.
- Leonard stays awake all night thinking about his confession. He's tormented by his imagination, and eventually gets up to go out, telling Jacky that he'll be back soon.
- Leonard takes a train to Hilton overnight and reaches his destination in the morning. He feels more alive and optimistic in the countryside, far from the artifice of the city.
- Leonard reaches Howards End, and finds himself with Margaret and some other people. He is totally disoriented and confused – and is attacked by a strange man, who grabs him by the collar and says that he's going to thrash him.
- Confusion and violence ensues; Leonard is attacked by a bright stick, then collapses under a falling bookshelf. It's chaos.
- Charles, the attacker, declares that Leonard is faking – but, in fact, he's dead. They carry him outside.
- Margaret and Helen don't understand at first – they pour water on him, hoping to revive him. Miss Avery comes out and says that Charles murdered Leonard.

Chapter 42

- Rewind – we go back to Charles's encounter with Tibby. After leaving Ducie Street, Charles returns home, not knowing about the whole Helen-at-Howards End debacle. Mr. Wilcox is worried about Margaret, who hasn't come home (she and her sister are Howards

End, despite the fact that it's forbidden).

- Late that night, Charles and Mr. Wilcox have a heart-to-heart. Mr. Wilcox is worried about Margaret, and he's certain now that she's disobeyed him and gone to Howards End. He asks his son to go to the house the next morning and sort things out – basically, to kick Helen and Margaret out of Howards End. He's very clear in telling Charles *not* to use violence.

- OK, fast forward to the present moment – Leonard is dead by Charles's hand. Charles still thinks he didn't use violence. After all, he only struck Leonard with the flat part of the sword (the "bright stick" Leonard saw descending upon him). Miss Avery and Margaret both agree that Charles didn't use the edge, and he assumes that Leonard's death was due to a heart attack – of course, Charles himself isn't at fault.

- Charles stops by the police station in Hilton on his way back home and informs them that there's a dead man at Howards End. He tells them his part of the story is thanked, and goes home to tell his father.

- Charles informs Henry that he found Leonard at Howards End, and Henry is horrified – Charles makes it out as though Margaret and Helen were at fault somehow. The way he tells it, Leonard was in the last stages of heart disease, and just when Charles was going to show him what for, he just up and died.

- Mr. Wilcox goes along with the story until Charles mentions the sword, at which point, his father freaks out. It certainly sounds suspicious… It's unclear as to what the real cause of death was.

- Charles is anxious, and wonders what will happen in the aftermath of this scandal. Surely, they'll have to leave Hilton. He's just glad that, as he sees it, he's cleared the way for a breakup between Henry and Margaret.

- Mr. Wilcox casually mentions that he's going to go to the police station. (Dolly, who hasn't been told anything, wonders why – and we feel bad for her, the poor little fool.) Mr. Wilcox shows an unusual tenderness towards Charles, which makes his son suspicious.

- Mr. Wilcox returns, looking exhausted, and says that there'll be an inquest the next day, which Charles will have to attend. His son pompously and blindly assumes that he will naturally have to be there to act as the key witness.

Chapter 43

- Margaret is confused and horrified by all of this. How could any of this have happened? All Leonard wanted was to experience the beauty in the world, and this is what he got.

- Helen is also terrified, and all she can do is try to be calm and pick flowers to lay in poor Leonard's arms. Miss Avery tries to soothe her by reminding that Leonard never even knew about the child.

- Margaret answers the policemen's questions, and tells them that, though Charles may have provoked Leonard's heart attack, it was bound to happen by some means. The doctor agrees that this is how Leonard died.

- Margaret and Helen decide to return to Germany; Margaret hasn't heard from Henry, but assumes that their relationship is over for good. She peers into his future, imagining that he will recover from this incident, continue to prosper, and keep living life as he has so far.
- At this moment, she's called back to meet with him – Crane comes to pick her up and take her to Charles's house.
- Margaret informs her husband that she intends to go to Germany, and cannot forgive him for what he's said or done.
- Mr. Wilcox is exhausted, and they sit on the grass to talk. Margaret coldly returns the keys to Howards End, and refuses to hear what he has to say – now, she thinks she can see through his façade of kindness, and knows that it's just a masculine trick to make her swoon.
- She tells Henry that her life is with Helen now, and they're going to Munich the next day, right after the inquest.
- Henry informs Margaret that the verdict at the inquest is not going to be heart disease – instead, it will be manslaughter. Charles is going to go to prison. Henry is totally heartbroken.
- Margaret is not suddenly moved to change her mind – but as the day goes on, and Charles is sentenced to three years in prison, Henry himself breaks down. He gives himself up to Margaret, and she, relenting, takes him to Howards End.

Chapter 44

- Tom and Helen are discussing whether or not the baby (which has been born, obviously – some time has passed) is old enough to play in the freshly mown hay. Helen agrees, and the little boy runs off with the baby.
- Margaret and Helen agree that Tom and the baby will grow up to be lifelong friends, despite their difference in class.
- We find out that fourteen months have passed, and Margaret is still living at Howards End. It's summer now, and the fields and meadows are full of life.
- Helen speaks tenderly of Henry, and wishes he could be enjoying nature with them – unfortunately, his hay fever always keeps him inside. We learn that he's not doing so well; he's not ill, but he's exhausted and worried about the family, who's all there today for some reason.
- Helen admits to Margaret that she likes Henry now – things have clearly changed with all of them.
- Helen says that everything is peaceful now; she seems to have reached some new level of clarity. She says she will never get married. She feels terrible for the way she treated Leonard, and how she's forgetting him now.
- Margaret stops her sister from worrying and blaming herself, saying that we must all remember that we're all together in a bigger picture – humanity and the world – and she shouldn't be hung up on the individual.

- Helen tells Margaret that she has drawn everyone together by forgiving Henry and learning to understand each other. Margaret, it seems, has really become the new Mrs. Wilcox.
- The sisters look out over the fields and see London creeping towards them – suburbanization and its dangers is still a threat.
- Margaret is struck by the idea that everything is part of an evolving process; just because something is going strong now, it might not last. She feels hopeful, though, thinking that their home, Howards End, is both the past and the future.
- The Wilcoxes come out of their family meeting. Paul emerges first, and roughly tells Margaret to go in to Henry. He kicks the door on his way back in.
- Henry, Evie, and Dolly are inside. Some decisions have clearly been made: he wants to make sure that everyone is OK with the arrangements.
- The deal is, Margaret will get Howards End, and the children will get all of Mr. Wilcox's money when he dies; Margaret, in turn, will leave the house to Helen's son.
- Paul is feeling particularly insulted by the idea that the house will go to the illegitimate child, and Evie tries to calm him down before she leaves.
- As the children leave, Dolly mentions that Mrs. Wilcox had wanted Margaret to have Howards End all along – something nobody ever revealed to Margaret.
- Dolly, Evie, and Paul say goodbye and leave. Margaret asks Henry about Dolly's casual remark, and he tells her that his first wife had scribbled a note about Margaret and Howards End before she died.
- Margaret is chilled by this – it's too eerie. She reassures Henry that he hasn't done anything wrong.
- Henry, seeing Helen, Tom, and the baby, smiles for the first time and rushes out to them. Finally, we see a moment of joy and resolution.
- Helen cries out gleefully that the hay field has been mown, and there will be a bountiful crop that year.

Themes

Theme of Love

The message of *Howards End* is wrapped up in Margaret's mantra, "Only connect." What, you may ask, does this really mean? It's simple: love. This novel is all about love – all kinds of love: love between siblings, love between husbands and wives, love between kindred spirits, love of home, love for one's country…basically, love for anything and everything. Love may not be all you need (money's pretty important, too – check out another theme, "Wealth"), but it's pretty darn important. The fear that humans don't love each other enough anymore is pressing here, and the novel challenges us to try and love others and ourselves more.

Questions About Love

1. What different kinds of love do we see at work in the novel?
2. Is love truly the most important thing of all, or are there other possibilities presented here?
3. Do any of these characters actually achieve true love?
4. How might we define "love" for the different types of people we see here? For Margaret? For Helen? For Mr. Wilcox?

Chew on Love

Though the idea of love is a central theoretical concept in *Howards End*, the novel is largely concerned with its failures, rather than successes.

At the novel's end, the transcendent nature of love (and its capability for forgiveness) presents the only ray of hope for a changing England.

Theme of Society and Class

Society makes nothing but trouble for the characters in *Howards End*. The notion that each of us is socially predestined for a certain kind of life based on who our parents are and how much money we have (or don't have) is incredibly frustrating to accept, but in England in 1910 it's an unavoidable fact of life. Definition by class is an obstacle that all of the characters in Forster's novel face, and it's one that challenges what really matters, individual human relationships.

Questions About Society and Class

1. How is social class defined in Forster's novel?
2. We see a society in flux here – what kinds of factors are the cause of the sense of social discomfort or disruption?
3. Can one transcend one's social class? Do we see any examples of this?

Chew on Society and Class

Forster makes problematic the very concept of social class itself by revealing a society torn between two competing systems of hierarchy, those of liberalism and imperialism.

The end of the novel proposes a possibility of a utopian future for England, which can only be attained by the breakdown of social class.

Theme of Transformation

Change is scary. And it's all around us in the world of *Howards End*, which, as you might imagine, makes said world kind of a scary place. It's funny – while a lot of the novel is concerned with the coziness of domestic life and the comforting beauties of the English countryside, the rest of it is filled with a definite sense of menace; though there are things in everyday life that make living worthwhile, like a freshly-mown field or a leisurely lunch, we get the feeling that all of these things are somehow endangered by the social, economic, political, and even geographical changes facing the world Forster presents. England is faced with urbanization and modernity, and in the moment of the novel, it's about to fall off a precipice into a whole new era.

Questions About Transformation

1. What kinds of changes or transformations do we see in the society depicted here?
2. How do the different characters react to change? What is the dominant attitude towards it in the novel?
3. Is change always a bad thing in *Howards End*?

Chew on Transformation

Change (whether economic, geographical, or social) is overwhelmingly viewed as a negative quantity in *Howards End*, since it heralds the increasing isolation of individual human beings.

Two models of change are posed in *Howards End*: the first, the idea that change is inexorable and inevitable, is negative, while the second, in which the tide of civilization will someday return and undo itself, offers a kind of hope for the future. The end of the novel is unclear as to which model will ultimately rule.

Theme of Identity

One of the main questions *Howards End* asks us to consider is this: how can an English person go about being an English person in the England that the novel shows us? That sounds a little crazy, so we'll take a step back. The world of Forster's novel is rife with change and conflict, and each character we encounter is challenged by these changes and conflicts, not only on a political level, but on a personal one as well. It's up to them to decide, then, how best to reconcile their own personal desires and beliefs to the requirements of the society they live in – and it's a real challenge.

Questions About Identity

1. How much does one's social background predetermine identity in *Howards End*?
2. How are group identities described here – for example, family identities or national

identities?

3. Is it possible for one to change one's identity? Does anyone here actually undergo significant change in character over the course of the novel?
4. How much is identity linked to principle?

Chew on Identity

In *Howards End*, characters' identities are informed largely by their social circumstances, and the only way for any character to change is through a shift in social status.

Identity is far from individual in *Howards End*, and Forster problematically groups characters' personas by their identification with families or nations.

Theme of Dissatisfaction

Nothing is more frustrating than seeing your own limitations and *knowing* that you can't get past them – and that's exactly what happens to some of the characters in *Howards End*. Dissatisfaction is a product of many social factors here – class, gender, profession, among other things – and as a result, all of the characters are dissatisfied in some way. The modern world that Forster depicts, with its changing social norms and political conflicts, makes for a whole lot of unresolved personal troubles…some of which can never really be resolved, no matter how hard our characters try.

Questions About Dissatisfaction

1. Are any of the characters in *Howards End* truly *satisfied*?
2. Is there any suggestion of an ideal life in the novel, or are all different modes of living equally problematic?
3. Is dissatisfaction tied to financial instability?

Chew on Dissatisfaction

Dissatisfaction, in the world depicted in *Howards End*, is an inevitable condition of modern life.

In the capital-dominated, highly economized social world of Forster's novel, money is the only condition upon which happiness is based.

Theme of Men and Masculinity

E.M. Forster offers up all kinds of diverse examples of English manhood in *Howards End*, and it's up to us to pass judgment on all of them. Some are ridiculous, some intimidating, and almost none of them are satisfactory. Masculinity is one of the crises central to this novel, and

we have to keep asking ourselves what a "real man" *should* be like – what are the criteria in the world Forster creates, and are they actually useful?

Questions About Men and Masculinity

1. Though Mr. Wilcox is touted as the "real" man in the novel, Miss Avery scornfully suggests that he's not "a real soldier" – what does this mean for our image of masculinity here?
2. What does a character like Tibby represent? How does Tibby contrast with the other men we encounter?
3. What does English manhood as portrayed by the novel look like? What, according to the narrator, are its flaws in its current, modernized state?

Chew on Men and Masculinity

Though the Wilcox men are initially suggested as the reader's model for manhood, they are gradually revealed to be imperfect models, demonstrating that there is a lack of "real men" in the novel's vision of England.

All successful models of masculinity ultimately fail by the end of *Howards End*, suggesting that traditional male-dominated society is limping to an end.

Theme of Women and Femininity

If you think it's hard to be a strong, independent woman today, imagine giving it a shot in 1910. The female protagonists of *Howards End* are constantly faced with social pressures, censure, and frustrations that would drive any of us absolutely batty. They're living on the cusp of a world that looks more familiar to us, in which women are allowed to think and live for themselves, but occasionally they're slightly too far ahead of their time, which can make for a very frustrating experience. The novel challenges our perceptions of what traditional male-female relationships are, and how they might limit both genders in the long run.

Questions About Women and Femininity

1. Femininity is defined in many different ways by many different characters in this novel. What are some of these definitions?
2. How do the women in *Howards End* define themselves, versus how men define them?
3. Henry often comments that Margaret is not exactly what he thinks a woman should be, while she notes over and over again how he is a "real" man. How do definitions of gender function in this odd couple?

Chew on Women and Femininity

Forster consciously establishes Schlegel sisters as models of womanhood in the future – which makes their existence in the present of the novel extremely difficult.

By defining women as essentially emotional beings, Forster limits their ability to affect the economic world or social system of the novel.

Theme of Wealth

The brutal truth is, money matters. *Howards End* recognizes this horrible fact, though not all of its characters choose to admit it. The novel constantly demonstrates the need to balance ideals and practical concerns, and the main practical concern here is the acquisition, investment, and dispensation of funds. The problem, however, is the failure of some of the characters to see that worldly issues, like wealth, aren't necessarily incompatible with philosophical ones – the struggle they, and we, face throughout the book is how to reconcile these two sides of life.

Questions About Wealth

1. Does love or money win at the end of the novel? Or neither?
2. Does the novel ultimately pose any solutions to characters like Leonard and Jacky, or does it just leave them in the lurch?
3. Do we get any sense throughout the novel that the dire situation posed here – the rich stay rich, while the poor get poorer – will ever be improved?

Chew on Wealth

Though the end of *Howards End* is seemingly optimistic, it leaves the problem of financial disparity entirely unresolved; while Helen's child may be the spiritual heir to England, the Wilcox-Schlegel family's escape to the disappearing countryside fails to address the problems of social injustice created by the economic circumstances shown throughout the novel.

While *Howards End* appears to embrace an idealistic social stance – summed up in Margaret's mantra, "Only connect!" – it is fundamentally pessimistic about the social predetermination of wealth, which it views as inevitable and, furthermore, unstoppable.

Theme of Principles

Do you ever get yourself into situations where you *know* that you're making an argument that's going to come back and bit you in the you-know-where, but you do it anyway, just because you're too proud to admit that you're even a little bit wrong? Of course you have – we all do. And, because they're human, so do almost all the characters in *Howards End*. The whole novel is basically a long demonstration of the difference between principle and action, and the problems that can come from being inflexible about either of these things.

Questions About Principles

1. Does this story have a "moral"? Is there a guiding principle at work in this novel? If so, what is it?
2. Many of the characters we encounter are principled to a fault – how much idealism is too much idealism?
3. Is it possible to find a balance between the two extremes we see in the novel of Helen's strictly idealistic principles and Henry's intense pragmatism?

Chew on Principles

Throughout the novel, the notion of "proportion," though dismissed at first, emerges as the only way to balance idealism and the real world.

The novel's characters enact the need for a middle ground between high ideals and low desires through a spectrum of three characters, Helen, Margaret, and Henry; these characters function in relation to each other as representations of different attitudes.

Theme of Patriotism

Written in 1910, *Howards End* is a classic pre-World War I text, and its setup of English-German tensions is practically a textbook example of the kinds of national anxieties that led to the war. Though your AP Euro book might tell you that World War I started when Archduke Ferdinand assassinated, we can see from Forster's novel and other works of its time that the was basically *waiting* to happen for a long while; the political issues at hand are illustrated in a more individual, cultural light here as a personal struggle between Englishness and German-ness.

Questions About Patriotism

1. Does Forster privilege England over Germany? Or vice versa?
2. How are both of the competing nations here represented?
3. How does Forster use his characters to play out the national tensions between England and Germany?

Chew on Patriotism

While he avoids direct engagement with political situations, Forster's novel is largely concerned with the developing tensions between England and Germany as actors on the imperial stage.

Forster's depiction of the English and German character types in his novel encourages an idealistic revision of history – national conflict is resolved here through personal connections.

Quotes

Love Quotes

Margaret was silent. If her aunt could not see why she must go down, she was not going to tell her. She was not going to say "I love my dear sister; I must be near her at this crisis of her life." The affections are more reticent than the passions, and their expression more subtle. If she herself should ever fall in love with a man, she, like Helen, would proclaim it from the house-tops, but as she only loved a sister she used the voiceless language of sympathy. (2.7)

Thought: Early on, we see different kinds of love present in Forster's world; he's careful to show us the fine nuances between family love, romantic love, and love for other things, like one's country or home.

But the poetry of that kiss, the wonder of it, the magic that there was in life for hours after it--who can describe that? It is so easy for an Englishman to sneer at these chance collisions of human beings. To the insular cynic and the insular moralist they offer an equal opportunity. It is so easy to talk of "passing emotion," and how to forget how vivid the emotion was ere it passed. Our impulse to sneer, to forget, is at root a good one. We recognize that emotion is not enough, and that men and women are personalities capable of sustained relations, not mere opportunities for an electrical discharge. Yet we rate the impulse too highly. We do not admit that by collisions of this trivial sort the doors of heaven may be shaken open. To Helen, at all events, her life was to bring nothing more intense than the embrace of this boy who played no part in it. He had drawn her out of the house, where there was danger of surprise and light; he had led her by a path he knew, until they stood under the column of the vast wych-elm. A man in the darkness, he had whispered "I love you" when she was desiring love. In time his slender personality faded, the scene that he had evoked endured. In all the variable years that followed she never saw the like of it again. (4.5)

Thought: This long quote has a *lot* contained within it; first of all, Forster reminds us of what we all know – that we, humans (and more specifically, his English audience) are often wary of emotional moments. Though this is perhaps a wise way of looking at passion, it doesn't always work, and in our fervor for logic, we can forget how "love" can truly change lives forever. He then shows us how Helen's brush with passion changes *her* and her idea of romance forever.

Love, say the ascetics, reveals our shameful kinship with the beasts. Be it so: one can bear that; jealousy is the real shame. It is jealousy, not love, that connects us with the farmyard intolerably, and calls up visions of two angry cocks and a complacent hen. (16.47)

Thought: Love and jealousy – can the two really be spoken of separately? The narrator tries to distinguish between them here, saying that jealousy is a kind of animal instinct, while love is…well, something else, something more transcendent, apparently – but what?

An immense joy came over her. It was indescribable. It had nothing to do with humanity, and most resembled the all-pervading happiness of fine weather. Fine weather is due to the sun, but Margaret could think of no central radiance here. She stood in his drawing-room happy, and longing to give happiness. On leaving him she realized that the central radiance had been love. (18.24)

Thought: Love, here, seems like a force of nature, just as powerful and necessary as the sun – it's so natural, in fact, that Margaret doesn't even recognize it for what it is right away.

Margaret had often wondered at the disturbance that takes place in the world's waters, when Love, who seems so tiny a pebble, slips in. Whom does Love concern beyond the beloved and the lover? Yet his impact deluges a hundred shores. No doubt the disturbance is really the spirit of the generations, welcoming the new generation, and chafing against the ultimate Fate, who holds all the seas in the palm of her hand. But Love cannot understand this. He cannot comprehend another's infinity; he is conscious only of his own--flying sunbeam, falling rose, pebble that asks for one quiet plunge below the fretting interplay of space and time. He knows that he will survive at the end of things, and be gathered by Fate as a jewel from the slime, and be handed with admiration round the assembly of the gods. "Men did produce this," they will say, and, saying, they will give men immortality. But meanwhile--what agitations meanwhile! The foundations of Property and Propriety are laid bare, twin rocks; Family Pride flounders to the surface, puffing and blowing, and refusing to be comforted; Theology, vaguely ascetic, gets up a nasty ground swell. Then the lawyers are aroused--cold brood--and creep out of their holes. They do what they can; they tidy up Property and Propriety, reassure Theology and Family Pride. Half-guineas are poured on the troubled waters, the lawyers creep back, and, if all has gone well, Love joins one man and woman together in Matrimony. (20.1)

Thought: This is really just a big dramatic explanation of how much trouble love causes. It seems like it should be simple, and just between two people – but when marriage comes into it, it's actually a lot more complicated and difficult than it should be.

After dinner he asked Margaret if she wouldn't care for a turn on the Parade. She accepted, and could not repress a little tremor; it would be her first real love scene. But as she put on her hat she burst out laughing. Love was so unlike the article served up in books: the joy, though genuine, was different; the mystery an unexpected mystery. For one thing, Mr. Wilcox still seemed a stranger. (20.4)

Thought: Love, to Margaret, is a lot less extravagant than novels make it seem – rather, it's still exciting and strange, but not in the way she expects.

Only connect! That was the whole of her sermon. Only connect the prose and the passion, and both will be exalted, and human love will be seen at its height. Live in fragments no longer. Only connect, and the beast and the monk, robbed of the isolation that is life to either, will die. (22.3)

Thought: Margaret's beliefs are simple – we must all, as human beings, reach out to each other – and love each other. This, to her, is the only thing that can bring humanity together, and reconcile the warring sides of our desires (the physical and the intellectual).

How wide the gulf between Henry as he was and Henry as Helen thought he ought to be! And she herself--hovering as usual between the two, now accepting men as they are, now yearning with her sister for Truth. Love and Truth--their warfare seems eternal. Perhaps the whole visible world rests on it, and if they were one, life itself, like the spirits when Prospero was reconciled to his brother, might vanish into air, into thin air. (26.50)

Thought: This reflection begs us to wonder – how irreconcilable are Love and Truth? Is it really as impossible as it seems to both love someone and see them objectively?

She told herself that Mrs. Wilcox's wrong was her own. But she was not a bargain theorist. As she undressed, her anger, her regard for the dead, her desire for a scene, all grew weak. Henry must have it as he liked, for she loved him, and some day she would use her love to make him a better man. (28.14)

Thought: Margaret's love is enough to make her forgive Henry for his past wrongs, even through her mind tells her not to. Love, we see, is stronger than the intellect, even for the Schlegels.

Perhaps it was Helen's way of falling in love--a curious way to Margaret, whose agony and whose contempt of Henry were yet imprinted with his image. Helen forgot people. They were husks that had enclosed her emotion. She could pity, or sacrifice herself, or have instincts, but had she ever loved in the noblest way, where man and woman, having lost themselves in sex, desire to lose sex itself in comradeship? (40.2)

Thought: Helen's way of treating other humans is purely theoretical – they can influence her own life, but they don't seem to be as real as she is, somehow. Everything seems to revolve around her, which limits her from truly attaining the depth of feeling that others, including Margaret, feel.

"Here they are at last!" exclaimed Henry, disengaging himself with a smile. Helen rushed into the gloom, holding Tom by one hand and carrying her baby on the other. There were shouts of infectious joy.

"The field's cut!" Helen cried excitedly--"the big meadow! We've seen to the very end, and it'll be such a crop of hay as never!" (44.49-50)

Thought: Finally, a reconciliation – something productive has emerged from the tragedy at Howards End, and we discover a new sense of optimism in this reconstructed family of Helen, Margaret, Henry, and the baby. There's the prospect of a fertile, healthy new world, made possible by love and forgiveness, and we can only hope that it will come true.

Society and Class Quotes

"Esprit de classe"--if one may coin the phrase--was strong in Mrs. Munt. She sat quivering while a member of the lower orders deposited a metal funnel, a saucepan, and a garden squirt beside the roll of oilcloth. (3.27)

Thought: Despite the fact that Aunt Juley is fuming with rage, her class awareness is so strong that she won't let the lower class shopman see her in a state of emotional upheaval.

If only he could talk like this, he would have caught the world. Oh to acquire culture! Oh, to pronounce foreign names correctly! Oh, to be well informed, discoursing at ease on every subject that a lady started! But it would take one years. With an hour at lunch and a few shattered hours in the evening, how was it possible to catch up with leisured women, who had been reading steadily from childhood? (5.30)

Thought: Leonard is overwhelmed by the cultural wealth of the Schlegels – he is limited by his own social background, and feels as though he could never possibly catch up.

The boy, Leonard Bast, stood at the extreme verge of gentility. He was not in the abyss, but he could see it, and at times people whom he knew had dropped in, and counted no more. He knew that he was poor, and would admit it: he would have died sooner than confess any inferiority to the rich. This may be splendid of him. But he was inferior to most rich people, there is not the least doubt of it. He was not as courteous as the average rich man, nor as intelligent, nor as healthy, nor as lovable. His mind and his body had been alike underfed, because he was poor, and because he was modern they were always craving better food. Had he lived some centuries ago, in the brightly coloured civilizations of the past, he would have had a definite status, his rank and his income would have corresponded. But in his day the angel of

Democracy had arisen, enshadowing the classes with leathern wings, and proclaiming, "All men are equal--all men, that is to say, who possess umbrellas," and so he was obliged to assert gentility, lest he slipped into the abyss where nothing counts, and the statements of Democracy are inaudible. (6.2)

Thought: Poor Leonard. Forster condemns him to a lifetime of inferiority in this single paragraph, based on his problematic existence between classes – he's not at the extreme lower end of the spectrum, and is just genteel enough to have the desire to possess what the rich have…culture.

In the streets of the city she noted for the first time the architecture of hurry, and heard the language of hurry on the mouths of its inhabitants--clipped words, formless sentences, potted expressions of approval or disgust. Month by month things were stepping livelier, but to what goal? The population still rose, but what was the quality of the men born? (13.3)

Thought: The "she" here is Margaret, and her observations about the kind of people she encounters in the streets of rapidly changing London are provocative. She wonders (and we wonder with her) what sort of people modern urban life is producing – they barely sound like humans at all, the way they're described here. What is this doing to the overall shape of British society?

He did not want Romance to collide with the Porphyrion, still less with Jacky, and people with fuller, happier lives are slow to understand this. To the Schlegels…he was an interesting creature, of whom they wanted to see more. But they to him were denizens of Romance, who must keep to the corner he had assigned them, pictures that must not walk out of their frames. (14.3)

Thought: The Schlegels mean a lot more to Leonard than he does to them – to him, they're symbols of a kind of life he's only glimpsed, but can never really experience. The social gulf between them is impossible to bridge from his perspective, looking up from the abyss of poverty, but to them, it doesn't seem that vast.

A short-frocked edition of Charles also regards them placidly; a perambulator edition is squeaking; a third edition is expected shortly. Nature is turning out Wilcoxes in this peaceful abode, so that they may inherit the earth. (21.3)

Thought: This comical, yet rather horrifying vision of the junior Wilcoxes demonstrates just what we've been learning all the way through the novel – society is paving the way for more Wilcoxes, and they're the upcoming, hardy business class that's going to survive in the twentieth century.

But Leonard was near the abyss, and at such moments men see clearly. "You don't know what you're talking about," he said. "I shall never get work now. If rich people fail at one profession, they can try another. Not I. I had my groove, and I've got out of it. I could do one particular branch of insurance in one particular office well enough to command a salary, but that's all. Poetry's nothing, Miss Schlegel. One's thoughts about this and that are nothing. Your money, too, is nothing, if you'll understand me. I mean if a man over twenty once loses his own particular job, it's all over with him. I have seen it happen to others. Their friends gave them money for a little, but in the end they fall over the edge. It's no good. It's the whole world pulling. There always will be rich and poor." (26.36)

Thought: Leonard knows well what his fate is – he was born poor, and he always will be poor. He basically unknowingly reiterates a comment Mr. Wilcox made a while back (see "Wealth"), that society will always be divided into rich and poor; it's interesting to think that both of these men, despite their differences, have reached the same conclusion.

"No, let us go back to Helen's request," she said. "It is unreasonable, but the request of an unhappy girl. Tomorrow she will go to Germany, and trouble society no longer. Tonight she asks to sleep in your empty house--a house which you do not care about, and which you have not occupied for over a year. May she? Will you give my sister leave? Will you forgive her--as you hope to be forgiven, and as you have actually been forgiven? Forgive her for one night only. That will be enough." (38.24)

Thought: Helen's position in society – and society's unfair double standard towards women and men – both become apparent here. Helen is forced to leave England because she'll never be able to have a normal or socially acceptable life there again (but she can in Germany?), and even Henry, her brother-in-law, can't accept her and her situation. However, as Margaret points out, he himself was once in the same position as Leonard as the illicit lover of an unmarried woman, but he never took responsibility for it, and society, like Margaret, has forgiven him for it.

Tom held out his arms.

"That child is a wonderful nursemaid," remarked Margaret.

"He is fond of baby. That's why he does it!" was Helen's answer. They're going to be lifelong friends."

"Starting at the ages of six and one?"

"Of course. It will be a great thing for Tom."

"It may be a greater thing for baby." (44.4-6)

Thought: This friendship between Tom and Helen's child is a significant one – for one thing, as Helen comments, Tom (a mere country lad) could benefit from the friendship of a cultured, wealthy boy. Margaret, however, recognizes that being friends with Tom, who's a *real* person, not just an over-civilized rich kid, could actually benefit her nephew – who himself is interestingly a combination of Helen and Leonard, a kind of microcosm of a more integrated English society and a hope for the country's future.

Transformation Quotes

A block of flats, constructed with extreme cheapness, towered on either hand. Farther down the road two more blocks were being built, and beyond these an old house was being demolished to accommodate another pair. It was the kind of scene that may be observed all over London, whatever the locality--bricks and mortar rising and falling with the restlessness of the water in a fountain, as the city receives more and more men upon her soil. Camelia Road would soon stand out like a fortress, and command, for a little, an extensive view. Only for a little. Plans were out for the erection of flats in Magnolia Road also. And again a few years, and all the flats in either road might be pulled down, and new buildings, of a vastness at present unimaginable, might arise where they had fallen. (6.6)

Thought: The changeability of the urban landscape is one of the most prominent themes of *Howards End* – Forster is clearly concerned about the shifting physical world of London at his moment in time. The idea that the world as we know is always undergoing transformation is both fascinating and horrifying to both the narrator and the characters.

London had done the mischief, said others. She had been a kind lady; her grandmother had been kind, too--a plainer person, but very kind. Ah, the old sort was dying out! (11.1)

Thought: This passage, which refers to what the villagers of Hilton think upon Mrs. Wilcox's death, indicates that a certain order is passing away – the "old sort" referred to here is a kind of Englishness, a sort of good, solid, old fashioned national character that's endangered by modern urban life.

Looking back on the past six months, Margaret realized the chaotic nature of our daily life, and its difference from the orderly sequence that has been fabricated by historians. Actual life is full of false clues and sign-posts that lead nowhere. With infinite effort we nerve ourselves for a crisis that never comes. The most successful career must show a waste of strength that might have removed mountains, and the most unsuccessful is not that of the man who is taken unprepared, but of him who has prepared and is never taken. On a tragedy of that kind our national morality is duly silent. It assumes that preparation against danger is in itself a good, and that men, like nations, are the better for staggering through life fully armed. The tragedy of preparedness has scarcely been handled, save by the Greeks. Life is indeed dangerous, but

not in the way morality would have us believe. It is indeed unmanageable, but the essence of it is not a battle. It is unmanageable because it is a romance, and its essence is romantic beauty. (12.12)

Thought: This observation of Margaret's (then taken over and expanded on by the narrator) points to an interesting theme in this book – the idea that we can't really plan for life, for it never unfolds the way it should. Things change, but never exactly how we think they will, and no matter how prepared we are, we're never ready for them.

Concerts and plays swept past them, money had been spent and renewed, reputations won and lost, and the city herself, emblematic of their lives, rose and fell in a continual flux, while her shallows washed more widely against the hills of Surrey and over the fields of Hertfordshire. This famous building had arisen, that was doomed. Today Whitehall had been transformed: it would be the turn of Regent Street tomorrow. And month by month the roads smelt more strongly of petrol, and were more difficult to cross, and human beings heard each other speak with greater difficulty, breathed less of the air, and saw less of the sky. Nature withdrew: the leaves were falling by midsummer; the sun shone through dirt with an admired obscurity. (13.1)

Thought: If we're to believe the narrator, urbanization is a terrible thing; the city, though inevitable in its spread and transformation, is a negative force here that divorces humanity from Nature and everything natural with its constant, inhuman evolution.

The feudal ownership of land did bring dignity, whereas the modern ownership of movables is reducing us again to a nomadic horde. We are reverting to the civilization of luggage, and historians of the future will note how the middle classes accreted possessions without taking root in the earth, and may find in this the secret of their imaginative poverty. (17.2)

Thought: Here we find another comment on the ills of modern life, this time on the contemporary tendency to move around, rather than settling into a place forever. The narrator attempts to link the dullness of middle-class life with its lack of real connection to the places and things that furnish these lives.

"I hate this continual flux of London. It is an epitome of us at our worst--eternal formlessness; all the qualities, good, bad, and indifferent, streaming away--streaming, streaming for ever. That's why I dread it so. I mistrust rivers, even in scenery. Now, the sea--" (20.13)

Thought: Margaret is stressed out by the changing face of the city; she doesn't understand why mankind always has to demand change of itself. The metaphor of the sea, left unfinished, creates a different model – one in which the tide goes away but always returns.

Day and night the river flows down into England, day after day the sun retreats into the Welsh mountains, and the tower chimes, "See the Conquering Hero." But the Wilcoxes have no part in the place, nor in any place. It is not their names that recur in the parish register. It is not their ghosts that sigh among the alders at evening. They have swept into the valley and swept out of it, leaving a little dust and a little money behind. (29.25)

Thought: Wilcoxes are not made for permanence. They represent the kind of progress and change that Margaret's afraid of – they don't just settle in the same place, nor do they invest in *homes* the same way Mrs. Wilcox believed in Howards End, or that Margaret longs to have a house of her own forever.

Houses have their own ways of dying, falling as variously as the generations of men, some with a tragic roar, some quietly, but to an after-life in the city of ghosts, while from others--and thus was the death of Wickham Place--the spirit slips before the body perishes. It had decayed in the spring, disintegrating the girls more than they knew, and causing either to accost unfamiliar regions. By September it was a corpse, void of emotion, and scarcely hallowed by the memories of thirty years of happiness. (31.1)

Thought: The passing of Wickham Place is as tragic but inevitable as a human death – this description of the Schlegels moving from their childhood home is full of unease and more than a bit creepy. It contributes to the feeling of impermanence that pervades the whole text.

Margaret was silent. Marriage had not saved her from the sense of flux. London was but a foretaste of this nomadic civilization which is altering human nature so profoundly, and throws upon personal relations a stress greater than they have ever borne before. Under cosmopolitanism, if it comes, we shall receive no help from the earth. Trees and meadows and mountains will only be a spectacle, and the binding force that they once exercised on character must be entrusted to Love alone. May Love be equal to the task! (31.13)

Thought: Margaret thought that getting married would help her escape from the sense of things slipping away that has worried her all along, but now that she and Henry aren't settling down at Oniton, she still feels the inevitable change. Love, says Forster, is the only thing that can possibly save us all from the crumbling away of the world as we know it!

She lowered her eyes a moment to the black abyss of the past. They had crossed it, always excepting Leonard and Charles. They were building up a new life, obscure, yet gilded with tranquility. Leonard was dead; Charles had two years more in prison. One usen't always to see clearly before that time. It was different now. (44.10)

Thought: Margaret has finally come to accept the passing of time and the inevitable changes in her life – things are, of course, different after Leonard's death, and the new family that's emerged (Margaret, Henry, Helen, and the baby) is doing it's best to create a new life at Howards End, connected to the ancestral past (Mrs. Wilcox), but broken off from the events lost in the "black abyss" of the past year and a half.

"All the same, London's creeping."

She pointed over the meadow--over eight or nine meadows, but at the end of them was a red rust.

"You see that in Surrey and even Hampshire now," she continued. "I can see it from the Purbeck Downs. And London is only part of something else, I'm afraid. Life's going to be melted down, all over the world."

Margaret knew that her sister spoke truly. Howards End, Oniton, the Purbeck Downs, the Oderberge, were all survivals, and the melting-pot was being prepared for them. Logically, they had no right to be alive. One's hope was in the weakness of logic. Were they possibly the earth beating time?

"Because a thing is going strong now, it need not go strong for ever," she said. "This craze for motion has only set in during the last hundred years. It may be followed by a civilization that won't be a movement, because it will rest on the earth. All the signs are against it now, but I can't help hoping, and very early in the morning in the garden I feel that our house is the future as well as the past." (44.19-23)

Thought: Helen points out the fact that life as they know it at Howards End – which is somehow real, substantial, natural – is inevitably coming to its end with the spread of the industrial city. However, Margaret still holds out hope that the demon "civilization" can't possibly go on undefeated forever; she feels that somehow something that they have at Howards End (authentic Englishness? Nature? Or her idea of love?) will go on forever, despite the changing world.

Identity Quotes

So they played the game of Capping Families, a round of which is always played when love would unite two members of our race. But they played it with unusual vigour, stating in so many words that Schlegels were better than Wilcoxes, Wilcoxes better than Schlegels. They flung decency aside. The man was young, the woman deeply stirred; in both a vein of coarseness was latent. (3.32)

Thought: Family is a strong component of identity in this text; we see people classified by what their families represent. Ironically, we see that Wilcoxes and Schlegels are not so very different here, for both Charles and Aunt Juley give in to the same "vein of coarseness."

[Mrs. Wilcox] seemed to belong not to the young people and their motor, but to the house, and to the tree that overshadowed it. One knew that she worshipped the past, and that the instinctive wisdom the past can alone bestow had descended upon her--that wisdom to which we give the clumsy name of aristocracy. High born she might not be. But assuredly she cared about her ancestors, and let them help her. When she saw Charles angry, Paul frightened, and Mrs. Munt in tears, she heard her ancestors say, "Separate those human beings who will hurt each other most. The rest can wait." So she did not ask questions. (3.39)

Thought: Mrs. Wilcox has a kind of strange spiritual wholeness that none of the other characters possess; something about her connectedness with the land and with her English country roots gives her a kind of privileged instinctive knowledge.

Putting her head on one side, Margaret then remarked, "To me one of two things is very clear; either God does not know his own mind about England and Germany, or else these do not know the mind of God." A hateful little girl, but at thirteen she had grasped a dilemma that most people travel through life without perceiving. Her brain darted up and down; it grew pliant and strong. Her conclusion was, that any human being lies nearer to the unseen than any organization, and from this she never varied. (4.11)

Thought: Even as a child, Margaret has a kind of Mrs. Wilcox-like tendency to view people as individuals, rather than members of "organizations" like countries, and to imagine that we all have a unique understanding of spirituality that exists beyond the scope of what politics and history want us to think.

Mrs. Wilcox had no idea; she paid little attention to grounds. She was not intellectual, nor even alert, and it was odd that, all the same, she should give the idea of greatness. Margaret, zigzagging with her friends over Thought and Art, was conscious of a personality that transcended their own and dwarfed their activities. There was no bitterness in Mrs. Wilcox; there was not even criticism; she was lovable, and no ungracious or uncharitable word had passed her lips. Yet she and daily life were out of focus: one or the other must show blurred. And at lunch she seemed more out of focus than usual, and nearer the line that divides life from a life that may be of greater importance. (9.5)

Thought: This description, one of the odder ones in this novel, demonstrates Mrs. Wilcox's strange separation from the world – it's almost as if the narrator can't figure out how to describe her, except to tell us that she's so mysteriously, mystically amazing that there are no

words for it. She's just not of this world, even when she's in it.

To them Howards End was a house: they could not know that to her it had been a spirit, for which she sought a spiritual heir. And--pushing one step farther in these mists--may they not have decided even better than they supposed? Is it credible that the possessions of the spirit can be bequeathed at all? Has the soul offspring? A wych-elm tree, a vine, a wisp of hay with dew on it--can passion for such things be transmitted where there is no bond of blood? No; the Wilcoxes are not to be blamed. The problem is too terrific, and they could not even perceive a problem. (11.38)

Thought: Mrs. Wilcox's identification with Margaret is made clear in her final bequest of Howards End; the question of spiritual identity (of a person, of a house) is what's up for debate here. The metaphysical question, however, is lost on the pragmatic Wilcoxes.

"Henceforward I'm going my own way. I mean to be thorough, because thoroughness is easy. I mean to dislike your husband, and to tell him so. I mean to make no concessions to Tibby. If Tibby wants to live with me, he must lump me. I mean to love you more than ever. Yes, I do. You and I have built up something real, because it is purely spiritual. There's no veil of mystery over us. Unreality and mystery begin as soon as one touches the body. The popular view is, as usual, exactly the wrong one. Our bothers are over tangible things--money, husbands, house-hunting. But Heaven will work of itself." (23.1)

Thought: Helen declares her independence here, and it's a turning point in the novel – from here on out, she intends to do exactly what she pleases, and refuses to explain herself to anyone else.

"Oh! Well, I took you for Ruth Wilcox."

Margaret stammered: "I--Mrs. Wilcox--I?"

"In fancy, of course--in fancy. You had her way of walking. Good-day." And the old woman passed out into the rain. (23.36-37)

Thought: Mrs. Avery's confusion of Margaret with Mrs. Wilcox reminds us that the two women (the two Mrs. Wilcoxes, really) are growing closer and closer – Margaret is becoming more and more like her predecessor. Feel free to be a little creeped out. We are.

When a young man is untroubled by passions and sincerely indifferent to public opinion, his outlook is necessarily limited. Tibby neither wished to strengthen the position of the rich nor to improve that of the poor, and so was well content to watch the elms nodding behind the mildly embattled parapets of Magdalen. There are worse lives. Though selfish, he was never cruel; though affected in manner, he never posed. Like Margaret, he disdained the heroic equipment, and it was only after many visits that men discovered Schlegel to possess a character and a brain. (30.1)

Thought: Tibby takes Schlegel individuality to an extreme; he's more isolated than his two sisters in his true disregard for the rest of society. Unlike Margaret, he doesn't care about fitting in, and unlike Helen, he doesn't even care about rebelling in a dramatic way.

Why has not England a great mythology? Our folklore has never advanced beyond daintiness, and the greater melodies about our country-side have all issued through the pipes of Greece. Deep and true as the native imagination can be, it seems to have failed here. It has stopped with the witches and the fairies. It cannot vivify one fraction of a summer field, or give names to half a dozen stars. England still waits for the supreme moment of her literature--for the great poet who shall voice her, or, better still, for the thousand little poets whose voices shall pass into our common talk. (33.2)

Thought: One of the biggest unspoken (or partially spoken) questions in this book is that of England's identity – we have to wonder what England and its people have in store for them, and who will tell their stories.

Margaret's anger and terror increased every moment. How dare these men label her sister! What horrors lay ahead! What impertinences that shelter under the name of science! The pack was turning on Helen, to deny her human rights, and it seemed to Margaret that all Schlegels were threatened with her. "Were they normal?" What a question to ask! And it is always those who know nothing about human nature, who are bored by psychology and shocked by physiology, who ask it. However piteous her sister's state, she knew that she must be on her side. They would be mad together if the world chose to consider them so. (35.18)

Thought: The Schlegel identity is clearly outside the bounds of what the conventional (Wilcox) world thinks is "normal" – this is the moment of crisis for Margaret, where she's forced to choose between the life she's picked for herself with Henry, and her old identity as Helen's sister.

"I feel that you and I and Henry are only fragments of that woman's mind. She knows everything. She is everything. She is the house, and the tree that leans over it. People have their own deaths as well as their own lives, and even if there is nothing beyond death, we shall

differ in our nothingness. I cannot believe that knowledge such as hers will perish with knowledge such as mine. She knew about realities. She knew when people were in love, though she was not in the room. I don't doubt that she knew when Henry deceived her." (40.9)

Thought: Mrs. Wilcox (the first one) comes up again at the novel's end, as everything falls into place at Howards End – Margaret ponders the mystery of her identity, which seemed to merge somehow with everything else that was real in the world.

Dissatisfaction Quotes

He felt that he was being done good to, and that if he kept on with Ruskin, and the Queen's Hall Concerts, and some pictures by Watts, he would one day push his head out of the grey waters and see the universe. He believed in sudden conversion, a belief which may be right, but which is peculiarly attractive to a half-baked mind. (6.20)

Thought: Leonard is unhappy with his lot in life, but is curiously, rather desperately optimistic in a way – he thinks that he can somehow change himself wholly through his attempts to absorb culture.

Certainly London fascinates. One visualizes it as a tract of quivering grey, intelligent without purpose, and excitable without love; as a spirit that has altered before it can be chronicled; as a heart that certainly beats, but with no pulsation of humanity. It lies beyond everything: Nature, with all her cruelty, comes nearer to us than do these crowds of men. A friend explains himself: the earth is explicable--from her we came, and we must return to her. But who can explain Westminster Bridge Road or Liverpool Street in the morning--the city inhaling--or the same thoroughfares in the evening--the city exhaling her exhausted air? We reach in desperation beyond the fog, beyond the very stars, the voids of the universe are ransacked to justify the monster, and stamped with a human face. London is religion's opportunity--not the decorous religion of theologians, but anthropomorphic, crude. Yes, the continuous flow would be tolerable if a man of our own sort--not anyone pompous or tearful--were caring for us up in the sky. (13.2)

Thought: Here, the narrator depicts a kind of abstract dissatisfaction – this is different from Leonard's personal struggle, but is definitely related to it. He's talking about the dissatisfaction of modern urban life, in which humanity is subjected to a force alien to it – that of the city itself (in this case, London). There's something about the inhumanity of the city that forces mankind to seek solace elsewhere, like in the idea of God.

One guessed him as the third generation, grandson to the shepherd or ploughboy whom civilization had sucked into the town; as one of the thousands who have lost the life of the body and failed to reach the life of the spirit. Hints of robustness survived in him, more than a hint of primitive good looks, and Margaret, noting the spine that might have been straight, and the

chest that might have broadened, wondered whether it paid to give up the glory of the animal for a tail coat and a couple of ideas. Culture had worked in her own case, but during the last few weeks she had doubted whether it humanized the majority, so wide and so widening is the gulf that stretches between the natural and the philosophic man, so many the good chaps who are wrecked in trying to cross it. She knew this type very well--the vague aspirations, the mental dishonesty, the familiarity with the outsides of books. She knew the very tones in which he would address her. (14.3)

Thought: Margaret recognizes what Leonard himself might not – that he would be much, much better off living the life of the country, like his ancestors. However, driven by the desire for "culture," he's been warped and transformed into a kind of predictable mockery of the middle class.

"I never thought that walking would make such a difference. Why, when you're walking you want, as it were, a breakfast and luncheon and tea during the night as well, and I'd nothing but a packet of Woodbines. Lord, I did feel bad! Looking back, it wasn't what you may call enjoyment. It was more a case of sticking to it. I did stick. I--I was determined. Oh, hang it all! what's the good--I mean, the good of living in a room for ever? There one goes on day after day, same old game, same up and down to town, until you forget there is any other game. You ought to see once in a way what's going on outside, if it's only nothing particular after all." (14.16)

Thought: Leonard expresses here the frustration of being penned up in city life – his adventure in the woods showed him that there's more to life than the monotonous grind of work every day, even though civilization tells us that's what we should all be doing.

"But he must be one of those men who have reconciled science with religion," said Helen slowly. *"I don't like those men. They are scientific themselves, and talk of the survival of the fittest, and cut down the salaries of their clerks, and stunt the independence of all who may menace their comfort, but yet they believe that somehow good--and it is always that sloppy 'somehow'--will be the outcome, and that in some mystical way the Mr. Basts of the future will benefit because the Mr. Basts of today are in pain."* (22.18)

Thought: Helen is opposed to Henry and everything he represents; she sees his way of thinking of things as inhumane and falsely scientific. His point of view, as she sees it, fails to recognize how much harm it does to those discontented lower classes that they theorize about (like Leonard).

"Walking is well enough when a man's in work," he answered. "Oh, I did talk a lot of nonsense once, but there's nothing like a bailiff in the house to drive it out of you. When I saw him fingering my Ruskins and Stevensons, I seemed to see life straight real, and it isn't a pretty sight. My books are back again, thanks to you, but they'll never be the same to me again, and I shan't ever again think night in the woods is wonderful." (27.17)

Thought: Poor Leonard. After all of his troubles, he's ready to renounce his ambitions to culture and poetry and *real* life – he realizes that none of these things are possible without money. His new, harsher perspective on life is grim, to both Helen and us.

Leonard looked at her wondering, and had the sense of great things sweeping out of the shrouded night. But he could not receive them, because his heart was still full of little things. As the lost umbrella had spoilt the concert at Queen's Hall, so the lost situation was obscuring the diviner harmonies now. Death, Life and Materialism were fine words, but would Mr. Wilcox take him on as a clerk? Talk as one would, Mr. Wilcox was king of this world, the superman, with his own morality, whose head remained in the clouds. (27.20)

Thought: It doesn't matter how vast and sweeping Helen's fine moral ideas are – Leonard can't help but be worried about the small (but *not* insignificant) facts of his situation. He can't simply afford to indulge in poetic ideas…he just can't afford it.

Helen loved the absolute. Leonard had been ruined absolutely, and had appeared to her as a man apart, isolated from the world. A real man, who cared for adventure and beauty, who desired to live decently and pay his way, who could have travelled more gloriously through life than the Juggernaut car that was crushing him. (41.3)

Thought: Leonard's unhappiness seems to Helen to be all-absorbing – and romantic, in a warped way. It's his complete misery and the apparent injustice of his life, crushed by society's rules, that appeals to her, just for a moment.

Men and Masculinity Quotes

"Somehow, when that kind of man looks frightened it is too awful. It is all right for us to be frightened, or for men of another sort--Father, for instance; but for men like that! When I saw all the others so placid, and Paul mad with terror in case I said the wrong thing, I felt for a moment that the whole Wilcox family was a fraud, just a wall of newspapers and motor-cars and golf-clubs, and that if it fell I should find nothing behind it but panic and emptiness." (4.6)

Thought: Here, Helen proposes one of the problems of the novel – what makes a man a *real* man? The Wilcoxes, she suggests, are different from the sort of men they know, like their father or poor Tibby. There's something about the Wilcoxes that set them up as paragons of masculinity, and when that façade is cracked (by Paul's fear), it all breaks down.

Tibby was sensitive to beauty, the experience was new, and he gave a description of his visit that was almost glowing. The august and mellow University, soaked with the richness of the western counties that it has served for a thousand years, appealed at once to the boy's taste: it was the kind of thing he could understand, and he understood it all the better because it was empty. Oxford is--Oxford: not a mere receptacle for youth, like Cambridge. Perhaps it wants its inmates to love it rather than to love one another: such at all events was to be its effect on Tibby. His sisters sent him there that he might make friends, for they knew that his education had been cranky, and had severed him from other boys and men. He made no friends. His Oxford remained Oxford empty, and he took into life with him, not the memory of a radiance, but the memory of a colour scheme. (12.9)

Thought: This image of Tibby and his very special Tibby-ness is quite at odds with the other men – namely, the Wilcox men – that we encounter in the novel. Tibby provides a kind of foil to the image of strong, pragmatic, active manliness we see elsewhere; he's disconnected from everyday life to the umpteenth degree, and it renders him unmanly and oddly asexual.

I believe that in the last century men have developed the desire for work, and they must not starve it. It's a new desire. It goes with a great deal that's bad, but in itself it's good, and I hope that for women, too, 'not to work' will soon become as shocking as 'not to be married' was a hundred years ago. (13.7)

Thought: The speaker here is Margaret, and she's addressing the recalcitrant Tibby, who just doesn't want to have a job. Her comment makes clear her stance on men and their proper pursuits (work), but also on what she hopes women will become sometime soon – hardworking members of society.

It was hard-going in the roads of Mr. Wilcox's soul. From boyhood he had neglected them. "I am not a fellow who bothers about my own inside." Outwardly he was cheerful, reliable, and brave; but within, all had reverted to chaos, ruled, so far as it was ruled at all, by an incomplete asceticism. Whether as boy, husband, or widower, he had always the sneaking belief that bodily passion is bad, a belief that is desirable only when held passionately. Religion had confirmed him. The words that were read aloud on Sunday to him and to other respectable men were the words that had once kindled the souls of St. Catharine and St. Francis into a white-hot hatred of the carnal. He could-not be as the saints and love the Infinite with a seraphic ardour, but he could be a little ashamed of loving a wife. "Amabat, amare timebat." And it was here that

Margaret hoped to help him. (22.2)

Thought: Mr. Wilcox is the epitome of English stiff-upper-lippedness. He's not only closed off from his own inner life – he has fears that it's somehow wrong to have feelings and desires. Religion has done nothing but confirm this suspicion, and it's Margaret's job now to undo all of these accumulated beliefs.

"I am a man, and have lived a man's past." (26.63)

Thought: Whoa there, Henry. "A man's past"? Huh. This quote implies not only that all men have dark secrets (the result of, you know, sowing their wild oats, etc.), but furthermore, that it's *expected* of them in a way.

She tried to translate his temptation into her own language, and her brain reeled. Men must be different, even to want to yield to such a temptation. (28.5)

Thought: Margaret, thinking of Henry's transgression with Jacky, is horrified once again by how different men are – she's disgusted by his baser impulses.

"We fellows all come to grief once in our time. Will you believe that? There are moments when the strongest man--'Let him who standeth, take heed lest he fall.' That's true, isn't it? If you knew all, you would excuse me. I was far from good influences--far even from England. I was very, very lonely, and longed for a woman's voice. That's enough. I have told you too much already for you to forgive me now." (29.11)

Thought: Mr. Wilcox emphasizes the idea that *all* men, not just him, are inevitably led to temptation; there's something about male nature that's fundamentally different from women, as he tells it. Basically, he's saying that what Margaret can't possibly forgive him for is his maleness.

"I suppose so; but Ruth should have married a--no disrespect to you to say this, for I take it you were intended to get Wilcox any way, whether she got him first or no."

"Whom should she have married?"

"A soldier!" exclaimed the old woman. "Some real soldier."

Margaret was silent. It was a criticism of Henry's character far more trenchant than any of her own. She felt dissatisfied. (33.28-29)

Thought: Hmm. Miss Avery implies here that Mr. Wilcox is not a "real soldier" – or perhaps a real *man*. So…what is he, in her eyes? We have to wonder. We know that, in Margaret's opinion, Wilcoxes are necessary for the running of the world, but it's unclear if they are the real English people that the novel seems to be searching for.

"Not any more of this!" she cried. "You shall see the connection if it kills you, Henry! You have had a mistress--I forgave you. My sister has a lover--you drive her from the house. Do you see the connection? Stupid, hypocritical, cruel--oh, contemptible! --a man who insults his wife when she's alive and cants with her memory when she's dead. A man who ruins a woman for his pleasure, and casts her off to ruin other men. And gives bad financial advice, and then says he is not responsible. These, man, are you. You can't recognize them, because you cannot connect. I've had enough of your unweeded kindness. I've spoilt you long enough. All your life you have been spoiled. Mrs. Wilcox spoiled you. No one has ever told what you are--muddled, criminally muddled. Men like you use repentance as a blind, so don't repent. Only say to yourself, 'What Helen has done, I've done.'" (38.25)

Thought: Men are just the *worst*. Margaret, in a moment of transcendent fury, unleashes the truth upon Mr. Wilcox; he doesn't realize that his actions are far worse than Helen's. Because of the unfair difference in expectations of men and women, he has been allowed to prosper in society, while Helen is cast out of it.

Women and Femininity Quotes

The fun of it is that they think me a noodle, and say so--at least Mr. Wilcox does--and when that happens, and one doesn't mind, it's a pretty sure test, isn't it? He says the most horrid things about women's suffrage so nicely, and when I said I believed in equality he just folded his arms and gave me such a setting down as I've never had. Meg, shall we ever learn to talk less? I never felt so ashamed of myself in my life. I couldn't point to a time when men had been equal, nor even to a time when the wish to be equal had made them happier in other ways. I couldn't say a word. I had just picked up the notion that equality is good from some book--probably from poetry, or you. (1.7)

Thought: Helen, an independent woman, finds herself set back by the Wilcox certainty of masculine superiority – and, oddly, she finds herself enjoying it.

"I suppose that ours is a female house," said Margaret, "and one must just accept it. No, Aunt Juley, I don't mean that this house is full of women. I am trying to say something much more clever. I mean that it was irrevocably feminine, even in father's time. Now I'm sure you understand! Well, I'll give you another example. It'll shock you, but I don't care. Suppose Queen Victoria gave a dinner-party, and that the guests had been Leighton, Millais, Swinburne, Rossetti, Meredith, Fitzgerald, etc. Do you suppose that the atmosphere of that dinner would

have been artistic? Heavens no! The very chairs on which they sat would have seen to that. So with our house--it must be feminine, and all we can do is to see that it isn't effeminate. Just as another house that I can mention, but I won't, sounded irrevocably masculine, and all its inmates can do is to see that it isn't brutal." (5.44)

Thought: Margaret can't exactly explain why, but there's something about the Schlegel household that's eternally feminine. They're in direct opposition to the Wilcox household, in which the only female member, Evie, is as masculine as Tibby is feminine.

Year after year, summer and winter, as bride and mother, she had been the same, he had always trusted her. Her tenderness! Her innocence! The wonderful innocence that was hers by the gift of God. Ruth knew no more of worldly wickedness and wisdom than did the flowers in her garden, or the grass in her field. (11.5)

Thought: Mr. Wilcox's musings on the passing of his first wife indicate what he expects from women – at this stage in the novel, he seems to see them as children, whose innocence is their main virtue. How different is this naivety from the sheltered idealism of the Schlegel girls?

A younger woman might have resented his masterly ways, but Margaret had too firm a grip of life to make a fuss. She was, in her own way, as masterly. If he was a fortress she was a mountain peak, whom all might tread, but whom the snows made nightly virginal. Disdaining the heroic outfit, excitable in her methods, garrulous, episodical, shrill, she misled her lover much as she had misled her aunt. He mistook her fertility for weakness. (20.17)

Thought: Margaret is a woman grown into her own powers, even if Henry doesn't recognize it. She doesn't need to announce her "mastery" over herself and her future husband, the way a younger girl might; instead, she is confident in her own ways.

She knew of life's seamy side as a theory; she could not grasp it as a fact. (26.64)

Thought: Despite the fact that Margaret's a mature, self-sufficient lady, Forster still implies that she can't "grasp" the darker parts of life (like Henry's seedy past) – perhaps simply because she's a woman. In general, women in this novel (Margaret, Helen, Jacky) have difficulty really understanding the world of men and its grim facts of life.

But she crossed out "I do understand"; it struck a false note. Henry could not bear to be understood. She also crossed out, "It is everything or nothing." Henry would resent so strong a grasp of the situation. She must not comment; comment is unfeminine. (28.3)

Thought: Margaret is increasingly occupied by what is feminine or masculine – the problem of the relation between genders is a recurrent one here. Why should comment or analysis be seen as unfeminine? Henry seems to have a very clear idea of what women should or shouldn't do, and Margaret is well aware of this.

He was annoyed with Miss Schlegel here. He would have preferred her to be prostrated by the blow, or even to rage. Against the tide of his sin flowed the feeling that she was not altogether womanly. Her eyes gazed too straight; they had read books that are suitable for men only. And though he had dreaded a scene, and though she had determined against one, there was a scene, all the same. It was somehow imperative. (29.5)

Thought: Henry expects Margaret to be upset, like any normal woman, by the news of his infidelity. However, Margaret is *not* a normal woman, which irritates him. For him, she's too much like a man to be properly feminine – too educated, too perceptive – and we can tell that she doesn't fit in with the image of womanhood that conservative men like Henry believe in.

Man is for war, woman for the recreation of the warrior, but he does not dislike it if she makes a show of fight. She cannot win in a real battle, having no muscles, only nerves. Nerves make her jump out of a moving motor-car, or refuse to be married fashionably. The warrior may well allow her to triumph on such occasions; they move not the imperishable plinth of things that touch his peace. (31.6)

Thought: Men and women, women and men…there's nothing but trouble between the sexes here. Henry, and men of his ilk, have a kind of warped idea of women. As the narrator comments here, men ("warriors") just humor women, who are nervous but entertaining creatures. We have to wonder how serious this commentary is.

Wealth Quotes

Why did we settle that their house would be all gables and wiggles, and their garden all gamboge-coloured paths? I believe simply because we associate them with expensive hotels--Mrs. Wilcox trailing in beautiful dresses down long corridors, Mr. Wilcox bullying porters, etc. We females are that unjust. (1.3)

Thought: Helen, writing to Margaret from Howards End, expresses from the beginning the association of Wilcoxes with money – with a kind of ostentatious wealth. Helen sidesteps the Schlegels' own odd standpoint, saying that "we females" are unjust; what she really should say is that wealthy liberals of their kind jump to conclusions.

"You and I and the Wilcoxes stand upon money as upon islands. It is so firm beneath our feet that we forget its very existence. It's only when we see someone near us tottering that we realize all that an independent income means. Last night, when we were talking up here round the fire, I began to think that the very soul of the world is economic, and that the lowest abyss is not the absence of love, but the absence of coin." (7.16)

Thought: Margaret, speaking frankly to Aunt Juley, acknowledges what her sister and their liberal friends never will – that, despite the idealistic talk of the equality of classes, they all rely upon money for their happiness.

"Oh, how one does maunder on, and to think, to think of the people who are really poor. How do they live? Not to move about the world would kill me." (13.7)

Thought: Margaret is again made painfully aware of her own wealth while pondering the move from Wickham Place – the Schlegels, for all of their big talk, still live a life of incredible privilege.

"When your Socialism comes it may be different, and we may think in terms of commodities instead of cash. Till it comes give people cash, for it is the warp of civilization, whatever the woof may be. The imagination ought to play upon money and realize it vividly, for it's the--the second most important thing in the world. It is so slurred over and hushed up, there is so little clear thinking--oh, political economy, of course, but so few of us think clearly about our own private incomes, and admit that independent thoughts are in nine cases out of ten the result of independent means. Money: give Mr. Bast money, and don't bother about his ideals. He'll pick up those for himself." (15.3)

Thought: Yet again, Margaret comes out and stands up against what she perceives to be the naively idealistic notions of her sister and their friends, saying that if you really want to help a man pull himself up in the world (for example, Leonard), the only thing to do is give him cold, hard cash – it's enough to purchase things like ideas eventually.

"Helen wouldn't agree with me here," [Margaret] continued. "Helen daren't slang the rich, being rich herself, but she would like to. There's an odd notion, that I haven't yet got hold of, running about at the back of her brain, that poverty is somehow 'real.' She dislikes all organization, and probably confuses wealth with the technique of wealth. Sovereigns in a stocking wouldn't bother her; cheques do. Helen is too relentless. One can't deal in her high-handed manner with the world." (20.8)

Thought: Again, we see the difference between worldly Margaret and high-minded Helen – the younger sister fails to recognize the practical uses of wealth, even though she can only truly be herself *because* she's wealthy. It's a quietly elitist attitude.

"There always have been rich and poor. I'm no fatalist. Heaven forbid! But our civilization is moulded by great impersonal forces" (his voice grew complacent; it always did when he eliminated the personal), "and there always will be rich and poor. You can't deny it" (and now it was a respectful voice)--"and you can't deny that, in spite of all, the tendency of civilization has on the whole been upward." (22.15)

Thought: Henry's opinion is, once again, in opposition to the Schlegel perspective. He argues against Helen that disparity in wealth is inevitable – and, furthermore, that the world requires it to make progress.

"I'll stand injustice no longer. I'll show up the wretchedness that lies under this luxury, this talk of impersonal forces, this cant about God doing what we're too slack to do ourselves." (26.27)

Thought: Helen, with the Basts in tow, has just crashed Evie's wedding in rather an insane fashion. She's on an anti-Wilcox crusade to show the wealthy people of the world how irresponsible they are. However, her mode of doing so doesn't seem entirely effective – she just comes off as stark raving mad.

"I wish I was wrong, but--the clergyman--he has money of his own, or else he's paid; the poet or the musician--just the same; the tramp--he's no different. The tramp goes to the workhouse in the end, and is paid for with other people's money. Miss Schlegel, the real thing's money and all the rest is a dream." (27.16)

Thought: Leonard, unlike Helen, has come to understand that life is impossible without money – even dreams themselves are impossible without cold, hard cash.

Helen had begun bungling with her money by this time, and had even sold out her shares in the Nottingham and Derby Railway. For some weeks she did nothing. Then she reinvested, and, owing to the good advice of her stockbrokers, became rather richer than she had been before. (30.23)

Thought: After her money is rejected by Leonard, Helen freaks out and doesn't know what to do with it. Without meaning to, she ends up even richer than before, emphasizing the idea that in this world, the rich just get richer while the poor (Leonard and Jacky) get poorer.

...of all means to regeneration Remorse is surely the most wasteful. It cuts away healthy tissues with the poisoned. It is a knife that probes far deeper than the evil. Leonard was driven straight through its torments and emerged pure, but enfeebled--a better man, who would never lose control of himself again, but also a smaller, who had less to control. Nor did purity mean peace. The use of the knife can become a habit as hard to shake off as passion itself, and Leonard continued to start with a cry out of dreams. (41.2)

Thought: Leonard's guilt over the incident with Helen changes him forever (in a notable contrast to Mr. Wilcox, who never seems to feel real remorse about his dodgy past). We see that Leonard is ultimately "a better man," but at what cost? And what can it possibly gain for him?

The expedition to Shropshire crippled the Basts permanently. Helen in her flight forgot to settle the hotel bill, and took their return tickets away with her; they had to pawn Jacky's bangles to get home, and the smash came a few days afterwards. It is true that Helen offered him five thousand pounds, but such a sum meant nothing to him. He could not see that the girl was desperately righting herself, and trying to save something out of the disaster, if it was only five thousand pounds. But he had to live somehow. He turned to his family, and degraded himself to a professional beggar. There was nothing else for him to do. (40.5)

Thought: This is just another case of Helen hypocritically taking her own wealth for granted; ironically, she's the one who deals the Basts the final killing blow by "crippling" them with the cost of the Shropshire misadventure.

Principles Quotes

The energy of the Wilcoxes had fascinated her, had created new images of beauty in her responsive mind. To be all day with them in the open air, to sleep at night under their roof, had seemed the supreme joy of life, and had led to that abandonment of personality that is a possible prelude to love. She had liked giving in to Mr. Wilcox, or Evie, or Charles; she had liked being told that her notions of life were sheltered or academic; that Equality was nonsense, Votes for Women nonsense, Socialism nonsense, Art and Literature, except when conducive to strengthening the character, nonsense. One by one the Schlegel fetiches had been overthrown, and, though professing to defend them, she had rejoiced. (4.3)

Thought: Here we see the conflict between Wilcox principles and Schlegel principles begin. Helen is at first seduced by how very different the Wilcoxes are – she's so intrigued that all of her favorite issues initially fall by the wayside (as Margaret's will later).

"I've often thought about it, Helen. It's one of the most interesting things in the world. The truth is that there is a great outer life that you and I have never touched--a life in which telegrams and anger count. Personal relations, that we think supreme, are not supreme there. There love means marriage settlements, death, death duties. So far I'm clear. But here my difficulty. This outer life, though obviously horrid, often seems the real one--there's grit in it. It does breed character." (4.7)

Thought: Margaret articulates the difference between the interior Schlegel world and the world that everyone else exists in (the "outer life"). The problem of the novel is basically the need to negotiate between the interior and exterior, which proves to be extremely difficult to work out.

"Inexperience," repeated Margaret, in serious yet buoyant tones. "Of course, I have everything to learn--absolutely everything--just as much as Helen. Life's very difficult and full of surprises. At all events, I've got as far as that. To be humble and kind, to go straight ahead, to love people rather than pity them, to remember the submerged--well, one can't do all these things at once, worse luck, because they're so contradictory. It's then that proportion comes in--to live by proportion. Don't begin with proportion. Only prigs do that. Let proportion come in as a last resource, when the better things have failed, and a deadlock--Gracious me, I've started preaching!" (8.30)

Thought: Here, Margaret tries to explain her life philosophy to Mrs. Wilcox – she tries, it seems, to just be as kind and honest as possible, and to take things as they come. When she refers to proportion, she's basically rebelling against the Wilcoxian idea that one can figure everything out rationally and mathematically.

The Wilcoxes continued to play a considerable part in her thoughts. She had seen so much of them in the final week. They were not "her sort," they were often suspicious and stupid, and deficient where she excelled; but collision with them stimulated her, and she felt an interest that verged into liking, even for Charles. She desired to protect them, and often felt that they could protect her, excelling where she was deficient. Once past the rocks of emotion, they knew so well what to do, whom to send for; their hands were on all the ropes, they had grit as well as grittiness, and she valued grit enormously. They led a life that she could not attain to--the outer life of "telegrams and anger," which had detonated when Helen and Paul had touched in June, and had detonated again the other week. To Margaret this life was to remain a real force. She could not despise it, as Helen and Tibby affected to do. It fostered such virtues as neatness, decision, and obedience, virtues of the second rank, no doubt, but they have formed our civilization. They form character, too; Margaret could not doubt it: they keep the soul from becoming sloppy. How dare Schlegels despise Wilcoxes, when it takes all sorts to make a world? (12.3)

Thought: This, to Margaret, is what the Wilcoxes stand for – the "grit" and practicality of the real world. While the Schlegels live in their equally necessary sphere of ideals and intellectual principles, the Wilcoxes represent the flip side of that kind of life.

"What is the good of your stars and trees, your sunrise and the wind, if they do not enter into our daily lives? They have never entered into mine, but into yours, we thought--Haven't we all to struggle against life's daily greyness, against pettiness, against mechanical cheerfulness, against suspicion? I struggle by remembering my friends; others I have known by remembering some place--some beloved place or tree--we thought you one of these." (16.32)

Thought: Margaret, frustrated by Leonard's own frustration, tries to express her desire to infuse ideals into actual life, rather than keeping the two worlds separate. She had hoped that Leonard also wanted to rise above the humdrum drone of the everyday.

"My motto is Concentrate. I've no intention of frittering away my strength on that sort of thing."
"It isn't frittering away the strength," she protested. "It's enlarging the space in which you may be strong." He answered: "You're a clever little woman, but my motto's Concentrate." (22.5)

Thought: This is the essential difference between Henry and Margaret – he believes in focusing intently on his own goals and just seeing what he wants to see in the world (or rather, what's beneficial to him), while she thinks that looking outwards and making connections and observations about others is the best way to go through life.

"That there are two kinds of people--our kind, who live straight from the middle of their heads, and the other kind who can't, because their heads have no middle? They can't say 'I.' They AREN'T in fact, and so they're supermen. Pierpont Morgan has never said 'I' in his life." (27.3)

Thought: Helen, lecturing at Leonard, rails against the Wilcoxes and everything they represent – that is to say, a mode of life that's focused on the exterior (on money, on business, on politics) rather than the interior life, or the "I," as she calls it. The Pierpont Morgan she references here was a famous American financier of the nineteenth century.

"If we lived for ever what you say would be true. But we have to die, we have to leave life presently. Injustice and greed would be the real thing if we lived for ever. As it is, we must hold to other things, because Death is coming. I love Death--not morbidly, but because He explains. He shows me the emptiness of Money. Death and Money are the eternal foes. Not Death and Life. Never mind what lies behind Death, Mr. Bast, but be sure that the poet and the musician and the tramp will be happier in it than the man who has never learnt to say, 'I am I.'" (27.19)

Thought: Helen's refusal to believe in the power of money (despite the fact that she herself relies upon it for everything) shows just how naïve and idealistic she still is – she has the luxury to believe in the poetic vision that the artist and humane man will be happier in the long run because they truly live for themselves.

"So never give in," continued the girl, and restated again and again the vague yet convincing plea that the Invisible lodges against the Visible. Her excitement grew as she tried to cut the rope that fastened Leonard to the earth. Woven of bitter experience, it resisted her. (27.23)

Thought: Helen's attempt to break Leonard free from the shackles of his worldly concerns is bound to fail – after all, he's been shown nothing but rough treatment from the world, while she's been coddled all her life. How can she, with all her innocent, well-meaning idealism, possibly undo everything he's experienced?

As is Man to the Universe, so was the mind of Mr. Wilcox to the minds of some men--a concentrated light upon a tiny spot, a little Ten Minutes moving self-contained through its appointed years. No Pagan he, who lives for the Now, and may be wiser than all philosophers. He lived for the five minutes that have past, and the five to come; he had the business mind. (29.21)

Thought: Unlike Helen, who tries to see everything in terms of the big, cosmic picture, Henry sees everything from the small frame of his own concerns, both personal and financial. Time, for him, is rather limited in scope to his immediate past and immediate future. This is indicative not only of the way he deals with everyday life, but with capital-L Life in general.

Tibby was silent. Without intending it, he had betrayed his sister's confidence; he was not enough interested in human life to see where things will lead to. He had a strong regard for honesty, and his word, once given, had always been kept up to now. He was deeply vexed, not only for the harm he had done Helen, but for the flaw he had discovered in his own equipment. (39.4)

Thought: Tibby's own moral code is a matter of intellect – he has a certain belief in the concept of honesty, but he doesn't really have feelings or sympathy to match. For this reason, he's only partially upset that he's betrayed Helen's confidence, but mostly alarmed that his own system is not as watertight as he thinks.

Morality can tell us that murder is worse than stealing, and group most sins in an order all must approve, but it cannot group Helen. The surer its pronouncements on this point, the surer may we be that morality is not speaking. Christ was evasive when they questioned Him. It is those

that cannot connect who hasten to cast the first stone. (40.3)

Thought: Helen doesn't seem to fall into any conventional definition of morality – and the narrator throws the very identity of morality itself. What makes morality, and who defines it? Who can dare to speak for all of humanity, or even society? The narrator concludes that it is not those who are *part* of a community, but those who fail to connect with one that make accusations.

Patriotism Quotes

Mrs. Munt had her own method of interpreting her nieces. She decided that Margaret was a little hysterical, and was trying to gain time by a torrent of talk. Feeling very diplomatic, she lamented the fate of Speyer, and declared that never, never should she be so misguided as to visit it, and added of her own accord that the principles of restoration were ill understood in Germany. "The Germans," she said, "are too thorough, and this is all very well sometimes, but at other times it does not do."

"Exactly," said Margaret; "Germans are too thorough." And her eyes began to shine.

"Of course I regard you Schlegels as English," said Mrs. Munt hastily--"English to the backbone." (2.4)

Thought: Aunt Juley, who is herself "English to the backbone," immediately establishes the juxtaposition of England and Germany, which represents itself in her half-English, half-German nieces.

A word on their origin. They were not "English to the backbone," as their aunt had piously asserted. But, on the other band, they were not "Germans of the dreadful sort." Their father had belonged to a type that was more prominent in Germany fifty years ago than now. He was not the aggressive German, so dear to the English journalist, nor the domestic German, so dear to the English wit. If one classed him at all it would be as the countryman of Hegel and Kant, as the idealist, inclined to be dreamy, whose Imperialism was the Imperialism of the air. (4.9)

Thought: It turns out that the Schlegels are neither here nor there when it comes to nationality (though for a while in the middle of the novel they are divided, with Margaret coming out all English, and Helen on Germany's side). We also see that even if we try to class them as German, it's not exactly the kind of politicized German we imagine; rather they, like their idealistic father, are English by birth and Romantic by philosophy.

"Someone's got to go," he said simply. "England will never keep her trade overseas unless she is prepared to make sacrifices. Unless we get firm in West Africa, Ger--untold complications may follow." (15.13)

Thought: Mr. Wilcox is obviously thinking of the conflict between England and Germany that's almost to a boiling point – but, sensitive to the Schlegels' dual nationalities, refrains from coming out and saying it.

"One is certain of nothing but the truth of one's own emotions."

The remark fell damply on the conversation. But Helen slipped her arm round her cousin, somehow liking her the better for making it. It was not an original remark, nor had Frieda appropriated it passionately, for she had a patriotic rather than a philosophic mind. Yet it betrayed that interest in the universal which the average Teuton possesses and the average Englishman does not. It was, however illogically, the good, the beautiful, the true, as opposed to the respectable, the pretty, the adequate. It was a landscape of Böcklin's beside a landscape of Leader's, strident and ill-considered, but quivering into supernatural life. It sharpened idealism, stirred the soul. (19.8-9)

Thought: Again, we see the difference between Germans and the English, as the narrator would have us believe – Germans are somehow more interested in the passions in a way that the English are not. This might explain why Helen, the more spiritually German of the two Schlegel sisters, is more idealistic and led by her emotions.

"If Wilcoxes hadn't worked and died in England for thousands of years, you and I couldn't sit here without having our throats cut. There would be no trains, no ships to carry us literary people about in, no fields even. Just savagery. No--perhaps not even that. Without their spirit life might never have moved out of protoplasm. More and more do I refuse to draw my income and sneer at those who guarantee it." (19.30)

Thought: Margaret's vision of Englishness is tied up in her understanding of the Wilcoxes – to her, they are the kind of hard-working people that England is founded on, and she refuses to think poorly of them, since they enable people like Helen and herself to live the lives they're accustomed to. Helen, on the other hand, doesn't think that this should excuse them for their flaws.

The sense of flux which had haunted her all the year disappeared for a time. She forgot the luggage and the motor-cars, and the hurrying men who know so much and connect so little. She recaptured the sense of space, which is the basis of all earthly beauty, and, starting from Howards End, she attempted to realize England. She failed--visions do not come when we try,

though they may come through trying. But an unexpected love of the island awoke in her, connecting on this side with the joys of the flesh, on that with the inconceivable. Helen and her father had known this love, poor Leonard Bast was groping after it, but it had been hidden from Margaret till this afternoon. (24.6)

Thought: It's only at Howards End that Margaret discovers a true, deep love for England – as she thinks, a "realization" of it that others have already felt. There's something about being in that place that puts her in touch more directly with her country, in a way that she's never felt before.

Here men had been up since dawn. Their hours were ruled, not by a London office, but by the movements of the crops and the sun. That they were men of the finest type only the sentimentalist can declare. But they kept to the life of daylight. They are England's hope. Clumsily they carry forward the torch of the sun, until such time as the nation sees fit to take it up. Half clodhopper, half board-school prig, they can still throw back to a nobler stock, and breed yeomen. (41.29)

Thought: The narrator's rather curious notion of Englishness emerges most clearly here, where he defines "England's hope" as the people of the countryside, who are still connected to the land and its spirit in a way that London businessmen never will be.

Plot Analysis

Classic Plot Analysis

Initial Situation
Wilcoxes vs. Schlegels: round one.
The tension between the two families begins right away, with Helen's brief and dramatic affair with Paul. Immediately, we see the Wilcoxes and Schlegels in conflict with each other – they're basically polar opposites, which makes them both attractive to one another, and repellent.

Conflict
Mrs. Wilcox leaves Howards End to Margaret.
Mrs. Wilcox and Margaret become friends, and the former tragically dies before their friendship can really flourish. In a seemingly inexplicable turn of events, though, Mrs. Wilcox leaves Howards End to Margaret, which puzzles and angers her husband and children. The Wilcoxes choose not to tell Margaret about this bequest, but it still sets up a sense of suspicion and fear with regard to the Schlegels, especially in Charles.

Complication
Henry and Margaret get married.
Despite their odd and complicated history, Henry is drawn to Margaret, and she to him. They decide to marry, which throws everyone into a tizzy – nobody else is pleased about this. Helen and Charles are especially unpleased. We can't tell how this is going to pan out; how can the Wilcoxes and Schlegels possibly interact as one single family?

Climax
Evie's wedding brings Helen back, with the Basts in tow.
All of the Wilcox-Schlegel tensions come to a head at Evie's wedding at Oniton Grange. Helen unexpectedly shows up with two unwanted guests, Jacky and Leonard, saying that they're starving and it's the Schlegel's fault. What she *really* means is that it's Henry's fault, since he gave the fatal advice to leave the Porphyrion anyway. It's revealed that that's not the only thing to blame Henry for – he also had a torrid affair with Jacky ten years ago, which may or may not have been the cause of his ruin.

Suspense
Helen is missing in action; everyone wonders if she's OK.
After the debacle at Evie's wedding, Helen goes off the map for a while. She doesn't want to see anyone in her family, and it seems like she's left England forever. Nobody can understand why – Margaret thinks that it's because she hates Henry so much, but that just doesn't seem like a satisfactory explanation.

Denouement
Helen is tricked into coming to Howards End, and her pregnancy is revealed.
Finally, we understand what Helen's been up to. The fact that she's pregnant makes everything fall into line, in a tragic way; all of the characters are brought back together a final time, in which the conflicts (Wilcox-Schlegel, Schlegel-Bast, and Wilcox-Bast) are all out in the open. Poor Leonard bears the brunt of it, and is killed as a result. However, though this isn't a happy unraveling of conflicts, it *does* allow for the whole world as we know it to be reevaluated.

Conclusion
In the aftermath of Leonard's death, a new order is established.
The fallout of Leonard's death by Charles's hand creates a new world for the Wilcoxes and Schlegels. Howards End ultimately ends up as their new home, and at the end, we see all of the loose ends tied up: the Wilcox children end up with all of the family money, while Margaret, Helen, and Helen's baby end up with the house.

Booker's Seven Basic Plots Analysis: Rebirth
OK, this seems like a stretch, but just go with us…

The hero falls under the shadow of a dark power…
The Schlegels and the Wilcoxes begin their odd relationship.

It's simple – when conservative Wilcoxes meet liberal Schlegels, conflict is inevitable. The "dark power" here could be seen as a couple of things – at this early stage, it seems to be the Wilcoxes themselves.

For a while, it seems to go well...

The Helen-Paul debacle blows over, and Margaret makes friends with Mrs. Wilcox
We wonder if perhaps Wilcoxes and Schlegels can coexist in the world. They're neighbors now, and it seems like things might actually work out. Margaret and Mrs. Wilcox form an odd bond, and their relationship makes it appear as though the breach between the two families is at least partially closed.

But eventually, it approaches again in full force...

Margaret and Mr. Wilcox get married.
Though it seems like the Wilcoxes and Schlegels seem to have broken off their association after Mrs. Wilcox's death, they find each other again after two years. Mr. Wilcox takes a liking to Margaret, resulting in their marriage. It looks to us (and to Helen) like Margaret has gone over to the dark side – she's fascinated by Mr. Wilcox's air of masculine ability and strength.

When it seems the dark power has completely triumphed...

Helen seems hopelessly estranged from her family. The Wilcoxes seem to have won for good.
After the horrible events of Evie's wedding, Helen banishes herself from England, and it seems like she'll never return. We wonder if the Schlegels will ever be reunited. Have the Wilcoxes and their mode of living triumphed over the romantic, idealistic Schlegels?

Along comes a miraculous redemption...

Back at Howards End, a new beginning.
After Society has basically crushed everyone – Wilcox and Schlegel alike – a new hope turns up just in time. Back at Howards End, Margaret, Helen, and Mr. Wilcox are all reunited. Helen's baby (notably, also Leonard's child) provides hope for a new kind of Englishness, one that's less torn apart by the problems of older social standards and structures. Even Mr. Wilcox has found a kind of release, and he and Helen are finally reconciled to each other.

Three Act Plot Analysis

Act I

Chapter 1-23. The Schlegel-Wilcox opposition is set up, and then cemented when Margaret decides to marry Henry; Helen comes out and says that she is breaking off from them.

Act II

Chapter 24-41. This act ends with the convergence of all of the bad things that have happened so far – Helen's pregnancy, Charles's Wilcoxian sense of propriety, and poor Leonard's final appearance. Of course, it all ends up at Howards End.

Act III
Chapter 42-44. After Charles inadvertently kills Leonard, the last couple of chapters tie up all of our loose ends – and present an opening into the future.

Study Questions

1. What is the significance of Howards End, the house? Why might Forster have named his book after it?
2. What do you think ultimately matters more in the world Forster presents, love or money?
3. Why does the country have such symbolic weight in the novel? What does the city represent? Is the city seen as uniformly bad, or does it have redeeming qualities?
4. What function do you think the character of Mrs. Wilcox plays? What does Margaret mean when she wonders if everyone else is simply a part of Mrs. Wilcox's mind?

Characters

All Characters

Margaret Schlegel Character Analysis

We can't help but picture Emma Thompson's earnest, endearing face when we think of Margaret Schlegel – the actress portrayed this character in the 1992 film version of Forster's novel, and, in our opinion, it was a job well done. Margaret, like the divine Emma, is characterized by her sympathetic qualities, her emotional honesty, and her clear-sightedness; however, before you start thinking that she's a too-good-to-be-true goody two-shoes, we should also add the fact that she's profoundly confused and torn between the various loves of her life, just like the rest of us. Margaret is a woman led by both her heart *and* her mind, and she strives to find perfect unity and balance in all of her relationships. However, this is easier said than done; in the end, it takes a whole lot of suffering for anyone we meet here to reach any level of resolution.

Margaret's struggles stem from her profound capacity for sympathy – she is uniquely able to see the good in everyone, and thus to extend her affection almost limitlessly. For this reason,

she's able to love both her passionate sister, Helen, and her repressed, emotionally thwarted husband, Henry, despite the fact that they're basically polar opposites. Margaret's creed, "Only connect," is the guiding message of the whole novel; Forster encourages us, like Margaret herself, to try and bring everything together in open relation, whether it be people or ideas.

As the book goes on, Margaret develops more and more into a kind of super-sympathetic, almost magical character; while she begins as a somewhat awkward intellectual, prone to putting her foot in her mouth, she grows into a more mature, understanding, and forgiving woman. The whole novel is basically the story of her gradual development, and all of the other main characters are ultimately drawn to her.

Margaret transforms into a kind of new incarnation of the mystical Mrs. Wilcox, who's able to bring her loved ones together and create a new, positive, productive kind of life for her family. Both of these women are, of course, tied intimately to Howards End itself, which figures as a crossroads between the past and the future. Margaret herself becomes a kind of bridge into the future; in the end, she has kept the family together (and, implicitly, England itself) and made it possible for her nephew, the next generation, to inherit a better world.

Margaret Schlegel Timeline and Summary

- Margaret receives a series of letters from Helen, who's visiting the Wilcoxes at Howards End.
- Alarmed by Helen's announcement that she's in love with Paul, Margaret lets Aunt Juley go to Hilton to sort things out. She finds out too late that it's all off. When Helen returns, they talk through the incident and put it behind them.
- Margaret strikes up a conversation with Leonard Bast at a performance of Beethoven's Fifth, then brings him home to pick up his umbrella, which Helen has accidentally stolen.
- The Wilcoxes move across the street, and Margaret befriends Mrs. Wilcox again, after an awkward start.
- Margaret attempts to draw Mrs. Wilcox into her circle of friends, but it doesn't work; the older woman seems almost to be of a different breed.
- Margaret and Mrs. Wilcox go Christmas shopping, and Mrs. W. invites her to Howards End for the evening. Margaret hesitates, says no, then at the last minute, dashes off to meet her friend at the train station.
- At the train station, the trip is prevented by the early return of Mr. Wilcox and Evie. Margaret doesn't get to see Howards End after all.
- Mrs. Wilcox dies, and Margaret attends her funeral at Hilton (though she doesn't see the house).
- Two years later, Margaret is occupied with trying to find a new house, since their lease on Wickham Place is up. Her brother and sister are no help at all.
- Schlegel life is interrupted by Jacky, then Leonard. Margaret and Helen both take an

interest in this young man with his big ideas.

- Margaret argues with her liberal friends and Helen about how important money is – she thinks that wealth is the first step in making a cultured, independent individual.

- Margaret and Helen run into Mr. Wilcox on the Embankment. He indicates that they should warn Leonard off of his current employer, the Porphyrion, and the sisters decide to do so. In the meantime, Margaret enquires about Howards End – she's still interested in the fate of the house.

- Margaret and Helen try to confront Leonard, with disastrous results. While he's visiting, Evie and Mr. Wilcox stop by and Leonard leaves in a fluster after Margaret comes out and tells him they're just trying to help.

- Evie (but really Mr. Wilcox) invites Margaret to a fancy, super-traditional lunch. She and Mr. Wilcox hit it off.

- The Schlegels go visit Aunt Juley, but as soon as they get there, Mr. Wilcox sends a letter offering them the lease on his house in London. Margaret goes back to town to take a look.

- Long story short, Mr. Wilcox proposes, and Margaret says she'll respond the next day by post.

- Margaret goes back to Aunt Juley's place, where she breaks the news to her family. Helen freaks out, but Margaret has her mind made up. She answers in the affirmative.

- Mr. Wilcox comes to see the Schlegels, and he and Margaret try to figure out their financial arrangements. Mr. Wilcox lets slip that the Porphyrion is just fine, which makes Helen and Margaret worry about Leonard. To prevent further argument, Margaret and Henry go to Howards End for the day to see Charles, Dolly, and the house.

- Margaret finally visits Howards End. Miss Avery mistakes her for Mrs. Wilcox for an eerie moment.

- Margaret goes to Oniton with her fiancé's family for Evie's wedding. The wedding is a success – until Helen shows up, Basts in tow.

- Margaret and Helen have a fight about how unreasonable Helen has been. Margaret attempts to clean up the mess her sister has caused, and inadvertently discovers that Henry had an affair with Jacky years ago. He calls off their engagement, feeling guilty and betrayed.

- Margaret sends away Leonard and Jacky, and tells Helen to stay (she doesn't). She decides to forgive Henry and marry him anyway. The couple is reconciled.

- Margaret and Henry are married, but Helen doesn't come. Margaret feels unsettled about how they don't have a consistent home – she'd thought they'd settle down somewhere right away.

- Miss Avery starts setting out the Schlegel's furniture at Howards End, and Margaret goes down to sort the whole mess out.

- Aunt Juley is unwell, and Margaret writes to Helen to tell her to come home. Helen refuses, unless it's an emergency. She comes to London, but won't see her siblings. Margaret, convinced by Henry, Charles, and Tibby, tricks Helen into coming to Howards End to pick up some of her things, and they plan to trap her there.

- Margaret ambushes Helen and discovers that she's pregnant. At Helen's request, she asks Henry if they can stay at Howards End for the evening, but he says no – this is a

moment of crisis for the couple.

- Margaret and Helen stay at Howards End anyway. Margaret decides to leave Henry and go away to Germany with her sister the next day.
- Leonard shows up and is accidentally killed by Charles; in the aftermath, Margaret decides to stay with Henry. They move to Howards End.
- Fourteen months later, Margaret, Henry, Helen, and Helen's baby have a new family unit. Finally, everyone Margaret loves has come together. It's decided that Howard End is her house, and she will pass it on to her nephew.

Helen Schlegel Character Analysis

Oh, Helen. Helen, Helen, *Helen*. Though we start out with friendly feelings for the younger Schlegel sister, it's impossible not to get exasperated by her headstrong behavior as the novel progresses. We have to give Margaret mad props for putting up with this pushy little sister; while Helen's certainly funny and lovable, she's also incredibly self-centered and self-indulgent at times. She, like Margaret, is independent, liberal, and extremely intelligent (not to mention argumentative), but unlike her older sibling, she doesn't exactly believe in the practical workings of the world. She's prettier and more charming than Margaret, and these things make her more popular in general…and they also allow her to drift through life in a kind of idealistic bubble. Helen's got money, looks, and brains, and all of this put together makes her a formidable young woman.

Helen, though she doesn't realize it, is spoiled in a very special way. Though she *thinks* she has the world figured all out, and that she's above petty concerns like money, she doesn't fully comprehend what Margaret increasingly does – that money is what enables her liberal, idealistic lifestyle. She's always spouting off poetic, abstract ideas about things like poverty and social injustice, but she doesn't see the irony here: Helen herself is rich, and she can never understand what it's like to be poor. For this reason, all of her philosophizing never really comes to anything, and when it comes down to actually helping people – the Basts – she proves to be a complete failure. If anything, Helen inadvertently causes their ruin, though she never fully understands that.

But Helen isn't *all* bad – she means well, after all. She's like that friend we all have who's totally involved with herself all the time; there's nothing *malicious* about it or anything, but she just can't really see outside the boundaries of the life she's always lived. Helen attempts to escape the repercussions of her decisions by fleeing England and gallivanting about Germany, which is posed as a kind of more liberal space. But, in the end, she can't stay away from her real home forever. Even though she's half German, her place is ultimately in England, at Howards End, with her family – Margaret, Henry, her baby, and even the difficult Tibby.

By the end of the novel, Helen has softened a little and, like everyone else, the tragedy that the

Wilcox-Schlegel family has come through together has forced her to grow up and see the world more clearly. The interference of real life with her philosophical ideals seems to have finally taught her a lesson, the hard way.

Helen Schlegel Timeline and Summary

- Helen visits the Wilcoxes at Howards End. She falls in love with the whole family temporarily, but Paul in particular.
- The thing with Paul only lasts about an evening – but by the time Helen can write to Margaret to say "never mind," it's too late. Aunt Juley arrives and causes a scene.
- Helen tries to explain herself to Margaret; her vision of love is a highly abstract one.
- Helen is unperturbed by the Wilcoxes' reappearance across the street from Wickham Place.
- At the Beethoven concert, Helen is overwhelmed by the music – she seems to *feel* music more than her siblings. She's so distracted that she walks off with Leonard Bast's umbrella, and he comes back with Margaret to fetch it.
- Helen goes on a trip to Germany with Frieda. There, she receives a marriage proposal, but turns it down.
- Helen returns from Germany, and Schlegel life goes on as usual for two years.
- Jacky shows up at Wickham Place and talks with Helen, who convinces her that her husband is not hiding out there. Helen is overwhelmed with delight at this comic figure, which strikes us as rather insensitive.
- The next day, Helen and Margaret are both fascinated by Leonard, who comes to explain his wife's visit. His tale of walking through the night intrigues Helen.
- Helen and Margaret are both concerned about Leonard, and discuss him with their friends, as well as with Mr. Wilcox.
- The sisters have Leonard over for tea, and try to tell him to quit his job at the Porphyrion. When he flees, Helen pursues him to try and talk some reason into him.
- Helen and her siblings go to visit Aunt Juley at Swanage. When Margaret goes off to London to see about the Wilcoxes' house, Helen warns her not to do anything foolish.
- Helen objects dramatically to Margaret's marriage to Henry. He basically represents everything she despises in the world.
- If Margaret must marry Henry, then Helen decides that she must cut herself free – she tells Margaret frankly that she still loves her sister, but she needs to do things her own way from now on…we wonder exactly what she intends to do.
- Helen turns down the invitation to Evie's wedding, but she crashes it anyway, with two "starving" guests in tow – the Basts.
- Helen charges in, claiming that she, Margaret, and Mr. Wilcox have destroyed Leonard and Jacky's lives, and that they owe it to the Basts to make it up. Margaret calms her down, and packs her and her "guests" off to the local hotel.
- Helen and Leonard talk over the situation and life in general, while they await word from

Margaret and Henry.

- Carried away by the perceived romance of Leonard's tragic situation, Helen sleeps with him, then flees, leaving him and Jacky with the bill.
- Helen goes to see Tibby, desperately flustered, and tells him to tell Margaret that she's gone away. She also instructs her unenthusiastic brother to give five thousand pounds to the Basts, which he reluctantly does.
- When the Basts refuse her money, Helen isn't sure what to do with it – so she reinvests it, and accidentally becomes even richer.
- Helen is on the run for a while – Margaret and Tibby can't pin her down, and she refuses to return to England from Germany. When Aunt Juley becomes ill, Helen comes back to London, but won't see her siblings.
- Lured by Margaret's trap, Helen shows up at Howards End. She and Margaret reconcile, and she tells her sister the whole story of her and Leonard, and her pregnancy.
- Helen begs Margaret to stay at Howards End that night.
- After Leonard's arrival and accidental death, Helen stays in England.
- Months pass. Helen has her baby at Howards End, and the Schlegels settle in there. Helen has changed a lot – she's even grown to care for Mr. Wilcox. It seems like she's finally grown up and learned to accept the real world, not just her out-of-reach ideals.

Leonard Bast Character Analysis

Leonard, as the narrator comments at one point, is more an idea than a person. He represents everything that's thwarted by modern life – he's a romantic and relatively intelligent young man who should be leading a healthy and happy life somewhere in the English countryside, but instead, he's trapped in a dead-end job in a dead-end city, London. Leonard is basically a picture of complete frustration; he's intellectually frustrated, sexually frustrated, and economically frustrated. That's a lot of stress for one dude, and it really shows in his prematurely aged demeanor. He's an all-around sad guy, and we have to feel bad for him, even if we don't find him particularly exciting or sympathetic.

Nobody finds Leonard particularly exciting or sympathetic, really – the Schlegels adopt him because of his interesting desires to escape the quiet desperation of his life, but he doesn't really live up to his potential for interest. The thing is, he's never *allowed* to live up to his potential because he doesn't have the most important ingredient – money. Forster uses Leonard to show us just how destructive poverty can be; being poor is what destroys Leonard's hopes and dreams, and his intellectual ambitions. It is what crushes him so completely, and that, in turn, is what draws Helen to him (it's totally warped, we know).

Leonard Bast Timeline and Summary

- Leonard encounters the Schlegel family at a concert. He chats with Margaret, and Helen unintentionally runs off with his umbrella.
- Leonard follows Margaret home to fetch said umbrella, and is rather taken aback by the madness of Wickham Place. He flees.
- Two years later, Leonard turns up once again, to explain why Jacky has visited Wickham Place. He describes his night of walking through the woods, and tries to tell the Schlegels about his desperate need to find more in life. They are fascinated.
- Leonard is summoned to tea with Helen and Margaret, who attempt to warn him off the Porphyrion. He is insulted, has a fight with them about their attempts to meddle in his life, and storms off in a huff.
- Leonard quits his job at the Porphyrion anyway, and finds a new one at a bank, at a lower pay rate.
- Things go from bad to worse for the Basts; Leonard is fired from his new job and can't find another.
- Helen "rescues" the Basts, and brings them to Evie's wedding. Everyone (including Leonard) is horrified.
- Leonard and Helen have an intense conversation, then end up sleeping together. Helen flees in the morning.
- Leonard feels terribly about what he's done – he resolves to find Margaret and confess everything.
- Leonard turns up at Howards End, only to find Margaret, Charles, and Helen. Charles strikes him with a sword, and he dies of heart failure.

Henry Wilcox Character Analysis

Mr. Wilcox is an Englishman through and through, with an upper lip so stiff you could use it as a cricket bat. He's the epitome of stoic, powerful, imperial manliness, which is why Margaret is so taken with him – and why her sister dislikes him so much for most of the novel. As a rich businessman with colonial ties (he runs some kind of rubber import business), we have to wonder exactly what Mr. Wilcox gets up to out in the world; as proved by the incident with Jacky in his past, it's not always morally correct.

It seems for most of the book that Mr. Wilcox has always been at a distance from his own feelings, and that he always will be. The only time that we see a crack in his façade in the early parts of the book is after his wife's death; he's deeply affected by the loss of Ruth, but he manages to pull himself together for the sake of his family and his business. He gets richer and richer as the novel proceeds, demonstrating what the narrator keeps emphasizing – people like the Wilcoxes are necessary for the smooth running of the world, and they will always prosper in

it. He, like the race he represents, is hardworking, unemotional, and, in some ways, simply unthinking – he doesn't mess around with feelings, nor does he spend much time analyzing himself or his decisions. He's always living on a business schedule, and that doesn't leave much time for a personal life.

Until, that is, he falls for Margaret Schlegel. The marriage of Wilcox and Schlegel is the union of opposite poles; Margaret is all about the interior life, while Henry is meticulously separate from his own interiority and only cares about the exterior. It's Margaret's mission to change this. She sees the capability for deeper caring in Henry, and she vows to make him a "better man" by bringing him more in touch with his own feelings. It seems for a long time that she's not succeeding, for, even after the incident with the Basts at Evie's wedding, Mr. Wilcox can't entirely come to terms with the black spots on his own past. However, by the end, personal tragedy finally cuts through Henry's thick armor of brusque capability. After Charles's fate is decided, Mr. Wilcox breaks down for the first time, and by the end of the novel, he's softened into a more loving, understanding man.

Henry Wilcox Timeline and Summary

- By coincidence, the Wilcoxes move in across the street from the Schlegels.
- Mr. Wilcox and Evie arrive home early from Yorkshire, preventing Margaret and Mrs. Wilcox from going to Howards End.
- Mr. Wilcox is distraught by the death of his wife. Upon receiving word of her last request (that Margaret get Howards End), he chooses to disregard it.
- Two years later, Mr. Wilcox runs into Margaret and Helen on the Chelsea Embankment one night, and he advises them to advise their friend (Leonard) in turn to clear out of the Porphyrion Company.
- Mr. Wilcox and Evie stop by Wickham Place when Leonard is there, and an awkward scene ensues. He clearly admires the way Margaret handles the situation.
- Via Evie, Mr. Wilcox invites Margaret to lunch at Simpson's. He is clearly interested in her, and wants to make sure she's not crazy.
- Mr. Wilcox writes to Margaret at Swanage to tell her that the Ducie Street house is to let.
- When Margaret comes to check out the house, Mr. Wilcox proposes.
- Mr. Wilcox goes to Swanage to see Margaret and her family, engagement ring in hand.
- Mr. Wilcox and Margaret pay a visit to Howards End to check out the property.
- At Evie's wedding, it emerges that Mr. Wilcox had an affair with Jacky ten years ago in Cyprus.
- Ashamed, Mr. Wilcox releases Margaret from her engagement. They patch things up, and the engagement is back on.
- The Wilcoxes are married soon thereafter. Mr. Wilcox refuses to live either at Howards End or Oniton, so they decide to move to Ducie Street while they wait for a new house in Sussex to be built.

- Margaret and Tibby seek Mr. Wilcox's help with Helen – upon hearing that she may be mentally ill, he takes control of the situation. The trap is laid at Howards End.
- Mr. Wilcox and Margaret go down to Howards End together to find Helen.
- Margaret explains Helen's situation to Mr. Wilcox; he's sure that they must find her lover and force him to marry her. Margaret asks only one thing – that they be allowed to stay at Howards End that night. Mr. Wilcox, who doesn't understand why Helen wants this, flatly says no – it would be an insult to his wife's memory. This is really rich coming from him, of all people.
- It seems like it's the end for Margaret and Henry.
- After the fatal incident between Leonard and Charles, Charles tells his father what happened. Mr. Wilcox, fearing that things are worse than his son thinks, goes to the police station to figure it all out.
- Mr. Wilcox tells Margaret that Charles will be accused of manslaughter. His heart is broken.
- Margaret takes Henry back, and the couple retreats to Howards End.
- At the end of the novel, Mr. Wilcox divvies up his fortune amongst his children and wife. The kids get all the money, but Margaret, and her nephew after her, get Howards End. It seems that Henry has changed a lot – he's slower, wiser, and seems a lot kinder after all of this heartache.

Mrs. Wilcox Character Analysis

If Leonard is more an intellectual idea than a real character, we might say that Mrs. Wilcox is more of a spiritual concept than a person. There's something otherworldly about her from the very first moment – when she notices somehow that Helen and Paul are "in love" – that continues to linger in the book in a loving fashion even after she dies. The other characters, namely Margaret, also notice this. Margaret and the narrator both comment consistently about the spectral presence of Mrs. Wilcox, who haunts the story and the house (Howards End) like a friendly ghost. She always seems to be around at key moments, like when Margaret's deciding to marry Henry, and somehow, we get the feeling that she's *involved* in the decisions made.

Creepy, right? We're not sure exactly what the deal is with Mrs. Wilcox and the strange, gentle, but urgent power she seems to exert, especially over Margaret. In fact, Margaret is more and more possessed by an odd kind of Mrs. Wilcox-iness over the course of the novel. Of course, she legally becomes the new Mrs. Wilcox when she marries Henry, but her transformation is more than just a name change; she takes on the same kind of grace and wisdom that her predecessor had. Miss Avery, Mrs. Wilcox's old friend, makes it clear in her eerie way that Margaret is the new Mrs. Wilcox in both name and spirit.

But what do we know about the *original* Mrs. Wilcox? The answer is simple: very little. She's always presented at a kind of distance from us, as though we *can't* really know her; we only get

snippets of her personal history, and we barely get to see her at all before she dies. Really, we rely upon the memories and musings of the other characters as they process her death and her continuing influence.

Mrs. Wilcox Timeline and Summary

- Mrs. Wilcox notices that Helen and Paul are in love.
- After the Wilcoxes move in across the street from the Schlegels, Mrs. Wilcox sends a friendly note to Margaret.
- Margaret rebuffs this offer of friendship. Mrs. Wilcox writes back to inform her that Paul is out of the picture, and she needn't worry.
- Margaret rushes over to apologize, and we find Mrs. Wilcox in bed for the day. We wonder if she's well.
- Mrs. Wilcox and Margaret go Christmas shopping together.
- Mrs. Wilcox is troubled by the idea that the Schlegels will be without a family home soon, and she keeps bringing it up while they are shopping.
- Mrs. Wilcox invites Margaret down to Howards End on the spur of the moment. Margaret says no, and Mrs. Wilcox goes a little cold.
- At home, Margaret changes her mind, and dashes to the train station, where she finds Mrs. Wilcox waiting for the train to Hilton.
- Before they can embark, Evie and Mr. Wilcox show up coincidentally, and everyone goes home. The trip to Howards End is delayed.
- Mrs. Wilcox dies and is buried in Hilton. Her last act is to change her will to give Howards End to Margaret.

Aunt Juley Character Analysis

Aunt Juley is the kind of comfortable, uncomplicated character we expect from Forsterian aunts. Aunts play an odd role in general in his novels – they seem to be ever present (often more present than mothers or fathers), and they're either consistently good or consistently annoying. Luckily for the Schlegels, Aunt Juley is the former, rather than the latter. She's a sweet lady, who seems primarily occupied with keeping her nieces and nephew happy, and (in her mind's eye) providing them with sound advice in the absence of their dead parents.

Aunt Juley doesn't have her own background or her own story; rather, she's just here as support for the Wilcox-Schlegel drama we see unfold in the novel. While she's inadvertently the catalyst for the whole business in the first place – after all, her altercation with Charles at Howards End basically sparks this whole sequence of events – her role after this initial moment is inessential. Really, she's most useful as a kind of cheerleader, both for the Schlegels, and for

England. She represents the most predictable kind of old fashioned English national character, the same way that Frieda represents Germany. The England we see in Aunt Juley is comforting, kind, a bit outdated, and, for lack of a better word, *auntish*.

Charles Wilcox Character Analysis

It's hard to put our feelings for Charles into language that's fit to be published by this fine website. Simply put, he's a fool – a pompous, thick-headed, stuff-shirted fool. And we hate him. Well, more specifically, we love to hate him. Charles is basically a collection of all of the traits that Forster sees as detrimental to the future of English manhood; he's imperious but imprudent, stubborn but stupid, and generally full of himself without any accomplishments to be proud of. He jumps to conclusions, then immediately jumps to actions (like killing poor Leonard) without ever thinking any of it through; as a man, he's constantly aware of the social demand that he *act* in some way, even when it's really the wrong response.

Tibby Schlegel Character Analysis

Tibby is perhaps the most remote of all of the many rather remote characters in *Howards End* – and intentionally so. As a consummate academic, he prefers to read about human behavior rather than experience it in the flesh, and all of his interactions reflect this perspective, even with his sisters (whom he loves, in his own special way – at a distance). Tibby is irritating, useless, pedantic, contrary, and dyspeptic (read: gassy), but all the same, we, like Margaret and Helen, simply can't stay angry at him; no matter how annoying he is, he's still kind of lovable in a weird way.

But why? Why shouldn't we just be able to dismiss Tibby as the most difficult member of a generally quite difficult set of siblings? The answer is simply that he doesn't exactly line up to our criteria of what makes a character (or person) good or bad in real life. Instead, his cartoonishly academic personality, likes, and dislikes make him into a bumbling, quirky outlet for comic relief. We are just as emotionally uninvolved with Tibby as he would be with us, and as a result, we're able to simply approach him as a kind of object of study.

Miss Avery Character Analysis

Miss Avery is more than a little creepy, and we're not sure how firmly she's planted on her rocker. She's the caretaker of Howards End, and was a close childhood friend of Ruth Wilcox's, despite the difference in their social statuses (Miss Avery and her family are of a lower class). She's convinced that Margaret, who she seems to see as the inheritor of her old friend Ruth's legacy, will come to live at Howards End, despite the fact that Margaret keeps

denying it, and she goes so far as to set up all of the Schlegel furniture up in the house while it's in storage there. She can clearly see the connection between Margaret and the first Mrs. Wilcox – we're not sure how – and she understands the need for Howards End to stay with someone who loves and cares for it.

Frieda Mosebach Character Analysis

Cousin Frieda, a delightful and cheerful young lady, really only serves one purpose: to represent the world outside England. Specifically, she represents Germany, the other side of the Schlegels' heritage. Her conflicts over nationality with Aunt Juley are only half-joking, and every time they argue playfully about whose nation is superior, it's always with a slight edge of seriousness. After all, let's not forget the fact that this novel was written in 1910, only four years before a certain Archduke was assassinated (leading to World War I) and the world changed forever.

However, Frieda certainly doesn't represent Germany as an evil, challenging nation – rather, we become quite fond of her, as her cousins are, and for good reason. She's fresh, funny, and generally a lovely person. This makes the whole pre-WWI "England is good, Germany is bad" dichotomy problematic. Instead, Forster invites us to consider the possibility that things aren't that simple: maybe England and Germany are both good *and* bad.

Jacky Bast Character Analysis

Poor Jacky. In the eyes of the other characters in the story, and in *our* eyes as the readers of the story, she doesn't amount to anything at all. Jacky is really just a symbol of all that's tragically wrong with the modern world – a woman destroyed by a male capitalist (Mr. Wilcox), destroyed by the unhealthy and disgusting city she lives in, and destroyed by her unfortunate social class. She's pathetic, stupid, and dull; basically, through no real fault of her own, she's ruined Leonard's life and her own. However, we can only feel bad for her, as Helen and Margaret do, because Forster implies that her fate was set in stone from the beginning – like all of the other characters here, she's a product of her class, time, and place.

Evie Wilcox Character Analysis

Evie, a fiercely healthy and athletic young lady, is really just summed up in those three words: fierce, healthy, and athletic. And we're not talking, like, *Top Model* "fierce" – rather, she's just determined to get her way. Not that Evie wants anything extraordinary…like her brothers, she's extremely conventional in her desires. She just wants to continue being wealthy, socially comfortable, and unembarrassed by anything. Is that too much to ask? In other words, Evie is

simply the female equivalent of Charles and Paul – and the exact opposite of Helen Schlegel.

Dolly Wilcox Character Analysis

Dolly is, for lack of a better word, kind of a bimbo. She's Charles's wife, and that's basically her entire role, both in life and in this novel. She's rather sweet and foolish, and is constantly putting her foot in her mouth. By the end of the novel, she's obviously had to grow up a little, what with Charles in prison and all, but she's still a total ditz; it's her unwitting slip of the tongue that lets Margaret know that Mrs. Wilcox gave her Howards End in the first place. Dolly might be seen as a figure for a super-conventional, silly young woman – a kind of foil to the non-silly young women of the Schlegel family.

Paul Wilcox Character Analysis

We don't really get to know Paul at all (and neither does Helen, really). We gather that he's kind of just a *guy* – charming in his masculine, Wilcox-ian way, but otherwise not too compelling. He's obviously sort of stuffy, the way his brother Charles is, and the way his father can be at times. We don't see him very often, since he's in Africa dealing with some kind of colonial business, which implicates him in the imperialistic kind of capitalism that all of his family is tainted by. Paul's basically a stock figure for the business class Edwardian young man, and his character really doesn't stand in for anything except convention.

Character Roles

Protagonist
Margaret Schlegel
Margaret, though only one of many possible protagonists in this novel, is the one who really stands out in our minds. She's undoubtedly at the heart of the action, and is also the most deeply developed, richly depicted character we encounter. Margaret is also the main psyche we explore here and, through her eyes, we see the main philosophical difficulty of the novel: how can one possibly reconcile the idealistic, castle-in-the-air fantasies of liberalism while also dealing with the down-and-dirty nuances of everyday life? Margaret's increasingly complex stance in between these two modes takes readers through the central journey of this text.

Antagonist
Henry Wilcox
Mr. Wilcox isn't a bad guy – don't let his label as the "Antagonist" here lead you to believe that. Rather, we might think of him more as a kind of oppositional force. If the Schlegels represent a

kind of liberal, idealistic, Romantic (and we *meant* that capital R) perspective, then the Wilcoxes are their opposites: Mr. Wilcox and his brood of young capitalists are conservative, pragmatic realists. However, as the novel goes on and the tragic events of the conclusion force everyone to reevaluate their positions, Mr. Wilcox's firm position breaks down, and he (like Margaret, and even Helen) ceases to antagonize.

Guide/Mentor
Mrs. Ruth Wilcox
Mrs. Wilcox serves as a kind of spiritual guide throughout the novel, and her ghostly presence is oddly more important than her short-lived physical one. She is the inspiration for Margaret's philosophical ponderings, and her spirit of acceptance and love for everyone is the guiding light in the long, dark night of this novel.

Foil
Helen Schlegel to Margaret Schlegel
Helen is a foil to her more measured older sister, Margaret. She's an uninhibited, wild, and self-indulgent version of Margaret, in whom we see romantic and liberal theoretical notions about society, life, and love all allowed to explode in every direction. Unlike Margaret, Helen doesn't think at all about the practical necessities of life, choosing instead to live entirely through her feelings and passions. This leads her to make a lot of mistakes – namely, sleeping with Leonard on a whim because she's taken by his state of utter desperation. Helen shows us what Margaret could be like if she weren't so plagued by things like money and convention…that is, the trappings of the real world.

Foil
Helen Schlegel to Henry Wilcox
Helen is also the polar opposite of Henry Wilcox, and their conflict is really the central problem of the book – Margaret is caught between these two extremes of liberalism and conservatism, and the project of the novel is to reconcile the two.

Informational Tool
Dolly Wilcox
Poor Dolly is always going around telling everyone things she's not supposed to tell them (like in the last chapter, when she spills the fact that Mrs. Wilcox wanted Margaret to have Howards End all along). She's just kind of a utilitarian character in life, as well as in the novel – her only real purpose is to be Charles's wife and have babies, and, for us readers, her only real purpose is to occasionally intervene and let fly some pertinent information. She's not really capable of anything else.

Character Clues

Direct Characterization

This is the simplest tool of all – Forster comes right out and tells us what people are like, and he even passes judgment in an overt and occasionally somewhat snippy manner. It's all just out there.

Family Life

We learn a lot from the three family units we encounter – the Schlegels, the Wilcoxes, and the Basts. None of these are exactly conventional, and their unconventionality is what renders them so unique. The odd no-parent, all-kids set up of the Schlegels alerts us to a certain ambiguity of maturity in all of the siblings, while the Wilcoxes, who are dominated by their father (largely from a financial perspective) are almost *too* concerned with the adult world of business and money. Finally, the Basts' incomplete "family" demonstrates the utter dissatisfaction of their lives; their everyday behavior expresses nothing but frustration and lack.

Thoughts and Opinions

Forster's third person narrator is comfortable moving in and out of the minds of his various characters, but he's more comfortable with some than others. We spend most of our interior time in Margaret's brain, through which we learn a lot about here, and also about the philosophical premises of the novel. The second most significant character we learn about through internal thoughts and opinions is Leonard Bast – the narrator's insight into his private world teaches us more than we could possibly figure out from his awkward, stunted exterior. We are also given the chance to visit Helen on occasion, and sometimes even minor characters like Tibby and Charles, though our views of how these characters work is more often than not simply validated by their inner workings.

Speech and Dialogue

The different modes of speech we encounter here, from Mr. Wilcox's brusque, somewhat condescending "man talk," to Leonard's awkward and halting conversation, to the endless flow of Schlegel babble all helps us understand the characters we encounter. Some, like Jacky, are hopelessly stunted; her language is repetitive and non-communicative (she mostly just says "What ho, Len!" and goes back to sleep), and is indicative of her low-level brain power. The Schlegels, however, constantly analyze and intellectualize everything, and therefore have to speak all the time – they can't help themselves. Speech can be viewed as a way into the characters' brain patterns, and "hearing" them talk is a clear way for us to view the ways in which they process life.

Education

Education and culture are hugely important here, and not in any oblique fashion – Forster comes right out and sets up the conflict between the characters that *care* about culture, art, and education (the Schlegels) and those who don't (the Wilcoxes). In between is Leonard Bast, who cares deeply about these things, but doesn't have the funds to attain them. It's clear that education here is a marker for a certain kind of social class – the liberal class whose wealth is inherited, not the business-centric, cash-earning new money. Tibby is the clearest example of the depiction of education here; he is totally defined by his over-educated life, and academia is

the be-all, end-all of his character.

Literary Devices

Symbols, Imagery, Allegory

"Home"

The idea of "home" is a major, *major* problem here. For the most part, our characters are uprooted and drifting – whether by choice or not. For some, like Henry Wilcox, houses have no sentimental value, and are just seen as investments to be turned into more money, while for others, like Leonard, urban poverty makes having a real home an impossible dream (we get the feeling that if Leonard's family had just stayed in the countryside, this might not be true – see "City versus Country" below). Home is the biggest problem for Margaret, though; she longs desperately for a house to call her own, and to feel truly *connected* to, and once the Schlegels are turned out of Wickham Place, she feels at a loss.

The only stable place any of the characters – or we, the readers, for that matter – can call home is Mrs. Wilcox's house, Howards End. After all, there's a reason the book is named after this remarkable place – it's the spiritual center of the England presented here, and it seems like Margaret's fate to finally inherit it in the end.

City versus Country

The dangers of city life concern the narrator of *Howards End* greatly, but they're not necessarily the fears of the big, bad city that we might expect – there's nothing dramatic about violent crime or inner city corruption. Rather, the novel is concerned with the less flashy, but no less alarming dangers of living in London: the damage it can do to one's character and personal relationships. The narrator and some of our characters are agitated by the continual flux of the city, in which things are constantly coming and going. London is portrayed like a kind of beast that consumes everything that crosses its path, from individual people to whole villages, and the threat of urban and suburban sprawl haunts the whole novel.

The country, on the other hand, is depicted as a space of real, proper Englishness – a place where the characters can truly connect with the land that they all come from. There's something *real* about the countryside (whether in Oniton or Hilton) that gets to both Margaret and the narrator – and, through them, to us, the readers. Country life seems to be somehow more substantial, natural, and, well, *human* than city life, and the relationships that people have both to each other and to the land itself seem more valuable there.

Nationality

There's not much to say about this concept – Forster is interested in the troubled relationship between England and Germany, and several of our characters play out these national roles

clearly. First of all, we've got the determinedly English characters, namely Aunt Juley and all of the Wilcoxes. The narrator, as well as Margaret, is curious about what makes England English – and who are the real English people, anyway? Part of Englishness is the imperial drive, represented by the Wilcox men, whose desire to conquer and pillage is barely concealed. Another part is Aunt Juley's pride in Englishness, which is demonstrated in her overflowing love for the subtle (but still remarkable), rather clichéd beauties of the English countryside. On the other hand, we have Cousin Frieda, whose pride in Germany is just as strong as Mrs. Munt's pride in England – Frieda represents a wholeheartedly good, though rather reductive, example of German patriotism.

In between these extremes, however, we have the Schlegels themselves – half-English, half-German, we see the conflict between nations played out in each of them individually, and ultimately in the clash between Helen and Margaret.

Setting

England around 1910 – principally London and Hilton, Hertfordshire
The big thing to notice with regards to setting here is the HUGE difference between city life and country life. The novel moves between urban and rural (and increasingly suburban) settings, and explicitly forces us to look at the problem of urban sprawl. Forster carefully situates his characters and readers in two "homes" – first, the Schlegels' house in Wickham Place, London, and second, in the Wilcoxes' house in the country, Howards End.

London is a place of chaotic progress in *Howards End*, and the way Forster depicts it, it's no surprise that our characters can't wait to escape the city. Sure, it's a place of cultural enrichment and sophistication, but it's also characterized by impersonal business relations and equally cold economic realities. The city is a place where both poverty and wealth are inescapable – and the disparity between the two is painfully marked. London is what ruins Leonard Bast, and also what drives Margaret Schlegel to long for a greater sense of human connection so desperately.

In counterpoint to this rather depressing vision of city life, we have an idealized – perhaps *over*-idealized – vision of the countryside. According to Forster, the country is the repository for all things old-fashioned and good; there are remnants out there of Ye Merry Olde Pre-Industrialized England. The narrator tells us frankly that people victimized by the city, like Leonard, would have been better off if they had just stayed in the pastoral settings of their ancestors. Poverty seems not to have a place in rural or village life, and there seems to be a greater sense of, for lack of a better word, a kind of primordial *Englishness* there.

Ultimately, the Schlegels and Wilcoxes retreat to the country to try and rebuild their families – and implicitly, to try and maintain the connection between England's past and future. We're not

sure how successful this venture will be, however; at the end of the novel, we see the ominous, rust-red glow of the city's lights impinging upon the rapidly suburbanizing countryside surrounding Howards End. Forster's novel leaves us uncertain as to what direction England is actually taking, and if there's any hope for the values of old England anymore.

Narrator Point of View

Third Person (Omniscient) – with the occasional odd lapse

For about 99.9% of *Howards End*, the narrative voice appears to be a somewhat sassy third person narrator, who can see into the hearts and minds of all of the characters (some more than others). The other .1% of the time, though, there's an odd "I" that shows up on the scene. This "I" is confusing – who is it? Is it some mystery narrator that we're just not supposed to wonder about? Is it Forster himself? The answers are not for us to know; rather, we just take it in stride. A better question is, what does it do for us, as readers? Basically, this unsettling gesture makes us question the objectivity of the narration throughout the whole novel – it reminds us that everything comes down to personal perspectives (what the Schlegels call the "interior" life), and that every single thing is viewed through our individual, unique, and incredibly human eyes.

Genre

Family Drama, Literary Fiction

While the genre of *Howards End* can certainly be said to be a family drama on a small scale – as in, it's about two very different families, the Wilcoxes and the Schlegels, and their difficulty reconciling with each other – we might also try and expand this term a little bit. The novel is both about the individual and the universal; while at first glance, the plot revolves around the relatively small and inconsequential lives of the very few characters we meet, its philosophical stakes are a lot higher. We might get a little loosey-goosey and say that this novel is also a drama of the *human* family and the need for sympathetic understanding.

On a less vague but still ambitious level, we could also say that it's specifically about the English part of that family tree; the novel is usually referred to as a "condition of England" novel, a genre in itself, in which an author approaches the question of the nation, attempting to figure out what makes England English, and if it can be improved upon – socially, politically, morally. Other famous "condition of England" novels you might have heard of include several of the works of Charles Dickens, especially *Oliver Twist* and *Hard Times*, and the novels of Elizabeth Gaskell, like *North and South*.

This gets us into the second genre we've chosen, literary fiction. This explicit project for the novel definitely means there's more at stake here than plot; this novel seriously works on so

many levels, not all of them simple or straightforward.

Tone

Alternately Rhapsodic and Dryly Humorous

Forster's tone is often an odd juxtaposition of highfalutin and quirkily humorous, with very little middle ground in between. *Howards End* is no exception; its tone alternates between the quite-serious and the quite-silly. Forster manages to express the dire philosophical and social troubles he's trying to communicate here, while all the while maintaining a healthy sense of humor. This makes for a novel that is both difficult and delightful by turns. It manages to encompass a weighty sense of the social troubles at stake, while still maintaining an oddly conversational, almost familial intimacy.

Writing Style

Realistic, Writerly, Super-Forsterian (whatever that means)

Forster's style is just so characteristically…Forster. His distinctive voice is unmistakable in its directness and ambition; we can practically see him straining to get across the philosophical angst he so clearly feels at times, and he reaches out towards us with such urgency, hoping to get us to reevaluate our lives and human relationships. He does this through both direct address and sneakier ways. His depictions of character are simultaneously sympathetic and unforgiving, and the realistic, sometimes cuttingly blunt detail with which he reveals his players to us communicates both tenderness and objectivity. His style as a whole might be summed up in those two words – he's tender without measure to his characters, and, in an interesting way, to us, his readers. But at the same time, he's not afraid to show them, and us, where they've gone wrong, and to sometimes come down quite harshly on them.

What's Up With the Title?

This name, though seemingly rather puzzling upon first glance, is actually thankfully straightforward: Howards End is a house. Not just any house, a very *special* house, that provides both the geographic and emotional center for the characters in this book. Its meanings are many and varied, and span both the literal and figurative; while Howards End is primarily a country home, one that is visited with fairly regular frequency by a variety of the characters in Forster's novel, it's also a metaphorical home. Howards End represents a kind of vision of family, of tradition, and of Englishness that runs through the entire book until, fittingly, we (and our main characters) take refuge there in the end.

What's Up With the Epigraph?

"Only connect…"

This phrase, a quote from the novel itself, is the guiding principle of its main character, Margaret (Schlegel) Wilcox. She longs for people to be able to reach out to each other and truly communicate – beyond superficial barriers like class or gender – and, as she says, "Only connect." We can also view this as a kind of pocket-sized version of Forster's philosophy; in a nutshell, he was obsessed with this idea of human connection and sympathy across boundaries of prejudice.

What's Up With the Ending?

The ending of *Howards End* contains multitudes – it seems incredibly simple in some ways (a family reunion, a plan for the future, a new hope – sounds almost like *Star Wars* when you put it that way), but in others, it's intensely complicated. Basically, we leave the Wilcox-Schlegels back at Howards End, the house that's at the heart of the whole novel, where they've all learned to make some kind of peace with each other, even if it's a somewhat grudging one. On one hand, there's a kind of unifying, cosmic justice at work here – as Dolly thoughtlessly comments, the first Mrs. Wilcox had wanted Margaret to have Howards End to begin with, and now, in the end, she gets it. On the other hand, there's an interesting sense that the old order (represented by the domineering, hyper-masculine, imperialistic Wilcoxes) has been fragmented, and either swept away or absorbed into the new, liberal, feminized world of the Schlegels.

It's an ending that is simultaneously unsettling and optimistic, in which we can only hope that the world that Helen's fatherless child will venture into will be ready for him. The general idea is, a new kind of England has emerged out of the convoluted events of the novel, and is represented by Helen's baby, who's an ultimate combination of all of the different social classes and circumstances Forster throws together in the novel.

Did You Know?

Trivia

- The film version of *Howards End* won three Oscars, after being nominated for a whopping nine awards. (Source)

Steaminess Rating

PG

Sex is definitely present here – after all, a baby arrives on the scene, and its conception is definitely not immaculate – but it's always well hidden in the shadows. We gather that Jacky and Henry had a physical relationship, that Leonard married Jacky in order to, you know, make an "honest woman" out of her, and that Leonard and Helen did the deed, but other than that, we don't get any more details. And, honestly, we really don't need them; part of what makes the sense of transgression and repression here so fascinating is the air of secrecy and discretion that surrounds sexuality.

Allusions and Cultural References

Literary References

- Walter Savage Landor, *Imaginary Conversations* (2.13)
- Georg Wilhelm Friedrich Hegel (4.12)
- Immanuel Kant (4.12)
- Algernon Charles Swinburne (5.44)
- Dante Gabriel Rossetti (5.44)
- George Meredith (5.44)
- John Ruskin, *The Stones of Venice* (6.12-21)
- George Meredith, *The Ordeal of Richard Feverel* (14.7, 41.9)
- Robert Louis Stevenson, *Prince Otto* (14.9)
- E.V. Lucas, *Open Road* (14.11)
- Robert Louis Stevenson, *Vignibus* (14.14)
- Richard Jefferies (14.17)
- George Borrow (14.18)
- Henry David Thoreau (14.18)
- Friedrich Nietzsche (27.3)
- Bluebeard (27.3)
- The Erinyes/Furies (41.2)

Pop Culture References

- Ludwig Von Beethoven, *Fifth Symphony* (5.1)
- Johannes Brahms, Four Serious Songs (5.12)
- Edward Elgar, *Pomp and Circumstance* (5.17)

- Charles Gounod, *Faust* (5.26)
- Giacomo Puccini, *Tosca* (5.26)
- Richard Wagner, *Tannhauser* (5.26)
- Claude Monet (5.28)
- Claude Debussy (5.28)
- Richard Wagner (5.30)
- Charles Ricketts (5.39)
- Frederic Leighton (5.44)
- John Everett Millais (5.44)
- John Anster Fitzgerald (5.44)

Historical References

- Battle of Sedan, 1870 (4.12)
- Napoleon III (4.12)
- German Unification (4.12)
- Boer War (18.16)
- Napoleon (27.3)
- James Pierpont Morgan (27.3)

Best of the Web

Links

Only Connect!
http://musicandmeaning.com/forster/
E.M. Forster's (unofficial) web presence, devoted to the author and his works.

Pharos
http://www.emforster.info/pages/contents.htm
Another very dedicated fansite.

Emforster.de
http://emforster.de/hypertext/template.php3?t=main&c
A questionably German website (in English) with great commentary and bibliography resources.

Forster at the Modernism Lab
http://modernism.research.yale.edu/wiki/index.php/E.M._Forster

Sadly, this isn't some mad scientist's attempt to clone E.M. Forster and his modernist contemporaries. Instead, it's a useful wiki about his life and work.

Movie or TV Productions
The heavyweights…
http://www.imdb.com/title/tt0104454/
Anthony Hopkins. Emma Thompson. Helena Bonham-Carter. Vanessa Redgrave. This 1992 film version, which is chock-full of the cream of the British acting crop, is the real deal.

Documents
Howards End on Demand
http://www.gutenberg.org/etext/2891
Desperately need to look up that quote? Here's the full text version on Project Gutenberg.

According to the Experts…
http://www.literaryhistory.com/20thC/Forster.htm
Here's a collection of links to articles on Forster and his works.

Videos
You've read the book. Now…movie night?
http://www.youtube.com/watch?v=BbKBrY7uBhE
If you're interested, here's the original trailer for the 1992 film.

Images
A bit more romantic than we'd pictured it…
http://www.impawards.com/1992/posters/howards_end.jpg
Here's the rather swoony poster for the film.

We're not entirely surprised.
http://modernism.research.yale.edu/wiki/images/E.M._Forster.jpg
Judging from this book, E.M. Forster was a pretty serious guy. This picture proves our guess right.

Printed in Great Britain
by Amazon.co.uk, Ltd.,
Marston Gate.